7/31/10

Linda!

- Ernest

THE WAY OF A

WITH HER GROOM

"Love may come softly, but grief shatters our world and leaves the
heart lying punctured and gasping."
the honor... the happiness, the beauty... and the grace...
Templates of truth for the Bride of Christ. Triumph over tragedy!

ERNEST WITMER

WESTBOW
PRESS®
A DIVISION OF THOMAS NELSON
& ZONDERVAN

WestBow Press books may be ordered through booksellers or by contacting:

WestBow Press
A Division of Thomas Nelson & Zondervan
1663 Liberty Drive
Bloomington, IN 47403
www.westbowpress.com
1 (866) 928-1240

ISBN: 978-1-5127-2554-4 (sc)
ISBN: 978-1-5127-2555-1 (hc)
ISBN: 978-1-5127-2553-7 (e)

Library of Congress Control Number: 2015921452

Printed in the USA

WestBow Press rev. date: 2/26/2016

CONTENTS

PREFACE

Do you ever get tired of the way church is done? Does it bother you that the Bride of Christ is really not that beautiful anymore? What if we started making Him the center of our attention and affection again? What if we remarried the Bride to the Groom?

Brides are beautiful! I always thought my wife, Rachel, was the most beautiful bride I'd ever seen. On October 20, 1984, we got married and walked a most amazing journey for the next 28 years and 17 days. But on November 6, 2012, Rachel went home to be with the Lord, her eternal Bridegroom, her forever Husband JESUS. I wish I could have been there in heaven to see her fall into His arms that day as she slipped away from mine!

Rachel was also a beautiful portrait of how the Bride of Christ, the church, should honor her Bridegroom, Jesus. Now I was not a perfect groom and didn't love Rachel perfectly when she was here. Yet she still honored me and gave me leadership to her life as my wife. So much more should Christians, who are the Bride of Christ, honor Him because He is a perfect Bridegroom and loved us unconditionally with a sacrificial love by dying on the cross for our sins. Imagine that—a Bridegroom dying for his bride. Now don't you think He deserves some honor from us in return?!

This book is the story of how one bride, my wife Rachel, did just that and left a legacy of honor not only to me as her leader and lover in the flesh, but to Jesus the eternal Lover of her soul. In *The Way of a Bride with Her Groom,* you can read her story and fall in love with the Bride of Christ again. Rachel is regaled in Christ's royal presence today. And this is why I tell her story. All she ever wanted to be on this earth was mine. And all she ever wanted us to be was His! Because of such faithfulness, she is where she is today, high above us all in heaven with Jesus. But she is also famous here on earth within the hearts and memories of everyone who knew her. If you want to go where she went, follow her as she followed Christ, and you'll end up where she is.

FOREWORDS

We can only try to imagine the scene. Six thousand years ago, somewhere in the realm of the heavenlies, the One who is three, yet one, having conversation within himself, saying, "Let's create Ernest, let's create Rachel, each of them in our image, after our likeness." So God created them, male created He Ernest, female created He Rachel. And God breathed into Ernest and Rachel His very own breath, and they became living souls. And God saw Ernest and Rachel whom He had made and behold, they were very good.

Resembling the likeness of God, they functioned as spiritual, eternal, creatorial, relational, rational, volitional, and emotional beings. Giving and receiving was in their makeup. Ernest, the male one, the groom, in all his strength with passion and courage, created in part to pursue, to initiate, to provide and protect, to move into in order to bring life, to bring fullness to what is empty, to bring shape to what is formless, and to bring order to what is chaos. Rachel, the feminine one, the bride, in all her beauty, created in part to invite, to entice, to respond and receive, to nurture, to shelter and preserve in order to enable and prosper life. Masculinity and femininity, each in their own uniqueness, coming together to more completely and fully represent the One in whose likeness and image they were created.

My wife Edith and I have known Ernest and Rachel for many years. We always admired their walk with Jesus, the demonstration of their faith journey together and their love for the church. Realizing depravity affects us all, they certainly were not perfect in their representation of their Creator, yet we never questioned their love for Jesus or their commitment to, by the grace of God as well as they were able, show off together the love, the care, the life, and the heart of the One who created them after His own likeness.

Together they have raised a beautiful and godly family. It's hard to understand the early passing of Rachel, and we have grieved deeply the loss of those who loved her. We claim the grace of God for those left behind with yet an unfinished call and purpose to continue showing off the One in whose image they (we) are created.

In the journey with Ernest,
Loyal Bacher, friend and certified counselor

What is more intriguing than a good love story? Unrivaled in our world, the theme of the cosmic dance of the universe, a love story woos us to the mercy seat and assures the heart that we are safe at the throne of grace. Love is invitation wrapped in security, communion, and delight.

Ernest Witmer has a love story to tell, but like all stories the Lord writes, his story is unique and filled with unexpected turns. No one begins their story, their love-pursuit of a wife, with the expectation of loss, tragedy, and grief. Love may come softly, but grief shatters our world and leaves the heart lying punctured and gasping.

Rarely have I met a man more brave or more honest with himself and God, and with as much integrity in the face of searing and sudden devastation. The unique combination of a fatal accident and his son's wedding in the same week is not often designed by the Lord for any of us to endure, much less triumph over. Ernest's story is one of triumph in the midst of tragic loss.

Ernest's loss parallels the life of the patriarch Jacob. He can also say, "Rachel died … to my sorrow … on the journey … when there was still some distance to go" (Gen. 35:19; 48:7).

Ernest, there is also "some distance to go" in your journey. This sorrow is latent with design. You have been appointed by the Lord to understand the days we live in, to learn the ways of the Lord through sorrow, and to bring to the church wisdom imparted through the crucible of pain. There is an enemy who would seek to *dis-appoint* you, to steal and disqualify the divine *appointments* of your life. Your *appointment* book is written by the Lord for this new journey. See that you are not *dis-appointed* by the enemy, but rather energized by your call and divine destiny. May this love message, borne of agony, be the launching pad from which you fulfill this next season of your life message.

Mark Yoder, friend and licensed counselor

TESTIMONIES

There is something truly precious about having a friend to "do life with." Rachel was that person for me. Looking back, I suppose our friendship started out more as a mentoring kind of relationship, with Rachel giving of her time and energy to walk alongside of me, encouraging me towards maturity and health. Over time it grew into so much more, a true side by side in the trenches kind of friendship. What Ernest writes about her is true. She was a gift not only to him and to her children, but to the many lives that she touched as she endeavored to "do life well." I am honored to have been her friend and will miss her until I join her in Heaven.

—*Karen Layman, friend, International Falls, MN*

Rachel. My friend, child of God, soft spoken, a loving mother. Mentor to me in the way she did life. Always a smile to greet others to make them feel loved. Never quick to anger but slow to speak, offering kind words and advice, never judging. Happy to serve, never demanding, to be served. I am anxious to see her again.

—*Her friend in Christ, Vickie Bernard, next-door neighbor and friend,*
International Falls, MN

Ernest Witmer is a man who loves God and who knows what it's like to experience what for most of us would be the ultimate fiery trial. It is my prayer that God would use this book to minister comfort to others who find themselves in a similar place.

—*Ray Comfort, Best-Selling Author & Founder of Living Waters*

From the time we met Ernest and Rachel in 1988, we experienced them as warm, welcoming, deeply passionate, caring, and authentic followers of Jesus. It was obvious that their goal in life was to love Him and represent Him to everyone they met. When Rachel graduated to Glory in what seemed to us such an untimely death, we saw Ernest draw even closer to his Savior. Rather than allowing his loss to cripple him, he clung more firmly to the Rock of Ages. We bless and endorse his diligent efforts to glorify the Trinity in this poignant reflection on his bride and his Bridegroom.

—Darrell and Kathy Nisly, friends and confidantes, Believer's Fellowship,
Sioux Narrows, ON

My wife and I consider it a privilege indeed to have been friends and fellow workers with Ernest and Rachel. May the Lord be pleased to use this book to glorify Himself in strengthening marriages and building up the Church.

—Allen Roth, mentor, supervisor, DestiNATIONS International,
Brooklyn, NY

I went to a funeral yesterday, the funeral of our dear friend Rachel Witmer, wife of 28 years and mother of five children. After the official service, we gathered at the burial site and a minister had some words. As the sun began to set, the cemetery director then announced the service was concluded and there would be some heavy machinery to lower the casket into the grave ... but no one left.

As we all stood there watching Rachel's casket lowered into the ground, something happened that is likely to stay with me for the rest of my life. Next to the gravesite was a massive pile of dirt and Rachel's husband Ernest approached the attendant and asked if he could have some shovels. They quickly fetched a dozen shovels and Ernest and his children began to shovel what I thought would be a few ceremonial scoops of dirt. Just then, all the men stepped forward, and under the chorus of hymns and the diminishing light of the setting sun, they shoveled, scoop by scoop the entire mound of earth, filling up the hole in the ground where Rachel would lie. In life, her family and friends loved and cared for her, and so it was in death as we all reverently, lovingly, and respectfully laid our dear sister in the ground. Although we all knew Rachel was not there, but was with our Lord around the throne singing a song that only she knows, we mourned, wept, and rejoiced as heaven received one its own.

— Jordan Dayoub, pastor friend

DEDICATION

This book is dedicated to my children—Carita, Marcel, Asher, Kristi, and Christopher. I want them not only to remember their mother, Rachel, but I also want them to remember the values she cared for and the convictions she carried. Their mother was my bride and, in being so, she was a resplendent representative of the Bride of Christ.

The Scriptures are clear: someday Jesus Christ is going to actually return for His Bride, the church. I want each of my children and my children's children to be part of that great wedding day when they will meet their mother again, and "so shall we ever be with the Lord."

CHAPTER 1
Birth of a Bride

Rachel's Story

They were high school sweethearts from Dakota, Illinois—Rachel's parents were. Her father Ron Schrader played Ebenezer Scrooge in their 1948 high school play "The Christmas Carol," and even though he's been pinching pennies ever since, he best represents the converted Scrooge after the third visitation. Her mother, Marianna Graybill, was a sweet fifteen-year-old girl for whom Ron had to wait patiently to begin dating. (Shh! don't tell anyone, but her parents lowered her dating-age eligibility because they liked him so well.) Their dating became steady after her sixteenth birthday.

They said their I dos on December 17, 1954, and Rachel showed up exactly one year and six days later on December 23, 1955. She was one cute little bundle of black-haired beauty! Ron and Marianna were delighted! She was their first child and the first grandchild on the Schrader side.

Nine months after her death in 2012, Rachel's son Asher would become the father of her first grandchild, Kenaz, who is also the first great-grandchild.

Rachel as an infant.

Rachel was soon followed by three more sisters within five years and then a brother soon after she turned six. Her firstborn birth-order position within the family system was quickly embedded within her persona, both for good and for decades of struggle. The good, of course, was that she immediately obtained a keen sense of personal responsibility—for herself and for others. The struggle came because she grew up with an underlying sense that she was valued more for what she could *do* than simply for who she *was*.

To this day it grabs my heart when I remember the first time she told me this. She never saw it as a negative reflection upon her parents or her younger siblings but simply as the role she was called to fill. And it was only by the grace-filled ministry of the Holy Spirit and the encouragement of caring friends that she eventually was able to gain an original sense of the wonderful little girl she was ... just for being WHO she was in the way God made her.

On the other hand, the benefit of her birth-order struggle is that she was delivered from the child-centered atmosphere prevailing in many homes today. Many parents nowadays have been duped into thinking their homes need to be built around their kids instead of around the marriage relationship of parents who are both centered in Jesus. The difference between these two philosophies is often the difference between heaven and hell. Rachel began life knowing the world did not revolve around her. And nothing could have prepared her better for being the blessing she was to so many people throughout her lifetime. She was free to focus on others and was bound to be a blessing to everyone.

The top take-away from this early-on aspect of Rachel's life was to turn the stumbling blocks of life into stepping stones. Granted, perhaps her parents should have been more careful to make sure she felt fully loved without any performance at all, just the way God loves us. But in their common defense, think of what they were experiencing at the time, and what Rachel herself went on to experience as a mother: the completely overwhelming demands of parenting young children. Her parents were doing exactly what God had commanded young couples to do: "Be fruitful and multiply, and replenish the earth" (Gen. 1:28). Rachel had no say in her birth order. God simply gave it to her, and she embraced it well. She went on to become the big sister every one of her siblings loved and learned from. What a vacancy she left in the Schrader family when she was suddenly snatched away!

Rachel with her siblings on the last Christmas of her life, 2011.

Her Inspiration

The first woman was formed around the rib of her man. From there she became his complement, made to receive him … to multiply his life. So every woman since Eve is born by God's design, uniquely fitted to find fulfillment around her husband's purpose, even if he himself doesn't yet fully know what that purpose is. She helps him find it. But just as she was made with a built-in capacity to fail with a man who was paralyzed by silence, so every woman since is born into an Adamic, broken-down world of fallen family systems.

Men are called to reveal God in ways uniquely masculine. Today they have gathered their courage and locked horns with this, their toughest issue: reclaiming the full potential of manhood. But in the midst of the excitement—the meetings, rallies, seminars, and high-fives—something vital is missing. Rediscovering neglected Biblical data shows us a well-rounded vision for mankind that redeems men from the squeezed and slender view that feminism has locked them into. It's ok for men to speak—in fact, it's incumbent upon them to do so. It's not ok for them to remain silent! It's ok for men to lead and to lead like a man, not like a woman. And it's not ok for them to plod along like a steer with a ring in its nose putting one dutiful foot in front of the other, not daring to upset the heifers. Men need to deal thoughtfully and honestly with the ongoing struggles and difficulties they have in relationships. But it summons them to get beyond their paralyzing fear of failure in order to take bold risk-taking action, to connect with others at a deep spiritual level, and to get on with genuine, full-hearted living.

Rachel motivated me to be this kind of man. The power of her presence in my life propelled me toward the promised land of Edenic manhood. She did this by being fully feminine herself, not by trying to be like me, or by trying to make me like her. I'm not suggesting that those tendencies and temptations never existed. They did, just like they did for Adam and Eve in the original Garden of Eden. But we lived on the right side of redemption. We knew what we were looking for and where to find direction.

I was motivated by a woman totally committed to living the way God designed her to live. You see, when God created mankind, He made them in His own image, both "male and female created He them." It took both of us to picture perfectly the image of God for our children. Just like it took both of us to conceive them, it took both of us to provide them with living demonstrations of what God is like. When I tried to be her, or tried to get her to be me, the image was darkened. Or when she tried to be me, or tried to get me to be her, again the image became unclear and confusing to our children. It took both of us being who God made us to be in bearing His image.

The Bride of Christ

The birth of a bride is no small deal. Every bridegroom knows that. Where on earth would we as grooms be if our brides had not been born? We'd still be out wandering the planet in search of a better half. But here they are as gifts from God—divinely delivered, supernaturally arranged, and perfectly joined to us to further propagate our kind.

So it is with the Bride of Christ! She is God's idea: He is the One who brings her around, the One who makes it happen, the One who multiplies our life through her. Marriage is not an end in itself! It is the picture of something much greater than the mere meeting, merging, and mating of a man and a woman for themselves. Jesus Christ is the end of it all: He is the real Bridegroom, the real Lover, and the real Life-giver!

When a church is born, it is no small deal either. Her Bridegroom, Jesus, has been longing for her to show up. She is His passion; her arrival is His delight! His discovery of her draws back the curtain to a divine delivery room where God introduces to the universe the birth of a marriage made in heaven. Christ and His new bride take center stage every time a fellowship of believers is formed. There's been a waiting time of longing, a time of courtship, if you please, a time of dreaming about what it would be like to actually live together as one body. And now the time has come. A new church is born.

God uses Christian marriage and the subsequent Christian family to model what He's looking for in His own relationship with us. When Christian couples move into a community, the good folks of the community wake up to discover within the dynamics of these new neighbors' marriage relationships something to imitate. It draws them in, and they begin to realize that what they're actually drawn toward is not the mere reflection they see but the real substance behind the mirror image. An earthly marriage is beautiful, of course, and the relationship real—but the marriages on display in an early church plant are reaching beyond the norms of human interaction. They are functioning within the dynamics of a divine romance, even if the neighbors don't yet recognize it themselves.

Rachel's story teaches me that births matter! A bride born from the sweetheart love relationship of marriage is bound to thrive despite all natural odds stacked against her. Half of Rachel's life was preparation to be married to a guy like me at twenty-eight years of age, and the other half was to be my bride and everyday inspiration for the next twenty-eight years of married life together. Both the story of her birth and her inspiration as my bride are rich with meaning for the Bride of Christ. Her life was a life of worship, pointing everyone to Jesus, both in how she honored Him for who He is and for how she honored me for who I was. Both her reverence for Him and her respect for me were contagious in how they influenced the other brides around her.

Reflections in Marriage

What is the meaning of marriage? What did God have in mind when He took Adam's rib and created Eve around it, bringing them together in marriage? What did Adam mean when he said, "This is now bone of my bone and flesh of my flesh; she shall be called woman." Exactly what is it in a man that makes a woman? And what is it in their union that makes a marriage?

We don't get very far into the New Testament theology of marriage until we come across Ephesians 5, which outlines for us in colorful detail God's design for marriage. He stages it as a picture, a symbol of something greater, or as we're considering it here, a reflection. Now if you have a reflection of something, there has to be something else that is being reflected. There is something *real* on the one hand that is showing up as a *reflection* on the other hand. For example, consider Rainy Lake in northern Minnesota on a calm summer day, the peaceful stillness of the water reflecting perfectly the beautiful scenery along the shore, so much so that you can hardly tell which are the actual flowers and trees along the shoreline and which are merely reflections of those flowers and trees.

Similarly in Scripture we discover that marriage is a reflection, or to use the proper ecclesiastical jargon, it's an ordinance. An ordinance is an earthly sign with a heavenly meaning, or to say it another way, a physical symbol with spiritual significance. In other words, marriage is something on this earth that is intended to be a picture of something in heaven, something within this earthly framework illustrating something in the spiritual realm. Marriage is a type. It is the shadow of something much larger and more real than itself. And remember, shadows are always true to their substance! A reflection is always congruent to the real thing it is reflecting.

Now this may at first seem a little disappointing to those who are married to think that marriage is not an end in itself. I'm sorry, but that's all it is—just an earthly illustration. It is not the real thing in terms of heaven and eternity. The real thing is Jesus Christ and the relationship He wants to have with His people. Our marriages are pictures of that relationship. Now that's significant, isn't it? So maybe it's not so disappointing after all!

"How-Tos" For Couples

Recently, within a week's time, two fellows asked me, "How do I get in touch with my wife's heart?" For most of us guys, this is a deeply puzzling thing. We're much more used to thinking in terms of our heads or our bodies—not our hearts.

John Regier once told me I had an "intellectually locked heart." (It's one of twelve kinds of "locked hearts" he says one can have.) He was right. It made perfect *sense* to me when he explained it that way, and it *felt* right to Rachel. Notice the difference? To me it was about what made *sense*, but to her it was about how she *felt*. And my intellectually locked heart was not a good combination to have with the "neglected locked heart" my wife had. Regier's remedy for me was to take three pills: Relax, Feel, and Enjoy. When I began to take those pills, it helped our relationship a lot and Rachel was happy! (But that was *my* heart. Let's get back to the hearts of our wives.) "How," these guys asked me, "do I get in touch with my wife's heart?"

What I said to both of those husbands may sound overly simplistic, but I believe it really cuts to the chase of how we connect with our wives. What I shared with them comes from a life of loving, living with, and losing my wife. It's experiential stuff. I simply told those young men to pay attention to what makes their wives happy.

What is it that makes her really come alive with joy? Such happiness is a cheerfulness that comes from them feeling fully cherished as the unique treasure God made them to be. It's not academic. It's instinctive. It's a heart thing. For me to really care about Rachel's heart, I needed to care about her happiness. Because when you know what makes your wife happy in this way, you know where her heart is. And when you know where her heart is, move towards it, wherever it takes you!

These are the seven things that made Rachel happy. Check them out, fellows. They would probably make your wife happy too.

Relationship: Husbands, more than she loves you, she loves this.
Connection: Talk about yourself or don't bother getting married!
Openness: She is body modest, but soul naked.
Children: Give her as many of these as her heart desires.
Conversation: "Tender words, gentle touch, and a good [conversation]" –Bill & Gloria Gaither

Friends: Share these. What's hers is yours.
Family: This comes along with the marriage.
Plus Mystery: The wonder of it all.

To begin with, it was all about *relationship* … to feel connected emotionally. Rachel truly loved me, but even more than loving me, she loved our relationship. That is, she loved feeling connected to me emotionally. When I did things to improve that *connection,* it made her happy. Very happy! She also cared about ME as an individual. So it made her happy when I was willing to talk about myself too— to be open with her about my thoughts, how my day went, what I was feeling. My *openness* always made her happy even if what I revealed to her wasn't always happy stuff.

Another huge part of Rachel's happiness was her *children*. When I moved toward our children and spent as much time as I could with them— playing with them, reading to them, holding lengthy conversations with them, this also made her day. Her *friends* made her happy as well, so when I made her friends my friends, this again made her happy. The same with her parents and siblings—the more I showed interest in her *family* and moved toward them in practical everyday ways, the happier she was. Whatever made her happy, I learned to treasure.

So, what makes your wife happy? Does she get all excited about flowers? Then you get excited about flowers too—her kind of flowers. Is it yellow flowers or red? Whatever it is, get excited about it. What's her favorite flavor? Does she like vanilla, chocolate, or some other kind? Does she like to go to bed early and get up early? Go with her. Is she more of a night owl? Then try that. Does she like quiet evenings at home? Stay at home with her. Would she rather get out of the house and go on a walk, visit some friends, or even go shopping? Hike, visit, and shop with her.

Well, you might say, that's a sure way to spoil your wife! No, not a godly wife. Not Rachel, and I don't think other wives either. And even if we do spoil them, so what! Isn't that what wives are for, at least in part? I sure wish I could spoil mine some more! Jesus said, "Where your treasure is, there will your heart be also" (Matt. 6:21). Want to know your wife's heart? Think *happy*.

And you know what? I have the happiest wife now. She has every desire of her dear heart completely satisfied. And she is happy. Perfectly happy! That's why my heart longs for heaven too—the ultimate place of happiness!

CHAPTER 2

She Called Him Jesus

Rachel's Story

Rachel had a rapport with Jesus I admired. And it all began right there in those early years of her life. Sitting reverently on the couch beside her mom, she'd listen, leaning in to see the pictures in order not to miss a word from *Marian's Big Book of Bible Stories*. Being the oldest in her family, she was usually at least one spot down from her mother, if not two, depending on how many of her siblings were around at the time. Rachel had no memories of sitting on her mother's lap (again, that early-life calling of birth order), but she caught every word and hung onto them for dear life. Years later, she could still quote verbatim to her own children from *Ethel Barrett's Bible Story* records. Her dad would read to her, too, on Sunday afternoons while they waited after church for dinner to be ready.

Mom and Dad Schrader were often exhausted from the rigors of farming, homemaking, and childrearing, so the temptation was always there to provide mere distractions to the children while they caught up on their own self-interests or afternoon naps. Since they didn't have a television in their home or even videos to play, there was no such evasion—or invasion, however you might look at it—from Mr. TV. But still, they could have replaced themselves with babysitters or canned forms of entertainment for children. Yet they did not, and those spiritual investments on the part of her parents were not lost on Rachel. This is how she first heard the Name of Jesus and how she first came to yearn after Him.

Rachel, the firstborn, on her father's lap.

Rachel's biggest struggle throughout life was fear. Raw fear was first introduced into her little heart right there on the farm, in the form of big animals. In first grade, she was required to walk up the long lane from the farmhouse to Winneshiek Road to catch the school bus. On either side of the lane were beef cattle grazing without the restraint of fencing, because her dad had what they called a cattle-guard at the end of the lane. Rachel would literally tremble inside as she walked up through the cattle with them mooing and snorting and following her along. She also had to contend with these big animals when she performed her duties of scattering straw in their pens in the barn. The moment she'd begin to shake the straw apart, the steers would jump and dance around, nearly knocking her over and causing her to emotionally fall apart inside. Thirty some years later, her eight-year-old daughter Carita would inadvertently step into an opening in the haymow and fall down into those very same pens full of cattle. She came stumbling and crying out to Grandpa Schrader who chuckled at her mutterings about the cattle. But she declared to him, "Grandpa, it's NOT funny!"—sentiments no doubt stemming back to her mother's quivering heart.

Fear showed up in Rachel already as a toddler. One day she stepped onto a thick book lying on the living room floor, but now—how to get down? She stayed there hollering with fear and trembling until her mom came to her rescue and delivered her safely back off the book. I'd like to believe Rachel was operating from a prophetic sense of call and thought she was standing on top of a pile of books as high as the downtown skyscrapers of Los Angeles. In the four years and seven months that Rachel and I lived with our family here in L.A. before her death, we distributed over half a million books through the venue of Choice Books. If we were to stack those books in piles around the tallest skyscraper here in downtown Los Angeles, we would have fifteen skyscrapers worth of books that have gone out into the greater Los Angeles region. Maybe, just maybe, that day as a toddler, Rachel envisioned she was standing atop one of those tall piles of books.

Whether from the top of a thick book or from scary-acting cattle, or even a blistering hot stove pipe that angled frighteningly up through her bedroom, Rachel eventually learned to trust Jesus against the fears that threatened her little heart. She was His bride in the making. She gave herself in confidence to Him for what she did not know and gained what she had come to love in this Jesus her parents first told her about.

Her Inspiration

Looking back on Rachel's life, it's easy to see how her childhood experiences shaped who she became. But life is lived in the present, and only God knows the full end from the beginning. Rachel's early childhood events were being processed long before the dimensions of time and perspective had lent their wise influence. As the poet once said, "The best thing you have in this world is Today. Today is your savior. But it is often crucified between two thieves: Yesterday and Tomorrow."

God knew, and her parents believed, that taking the time to read Bible stories to Rachel as a child would profoundly influence who she would be as an adult. But Rachel's parents couldn't jump ahead in time and immediately cash in on the benefits. Nor could they stall backward in time and say, "If our parents had only spent more time reading these stories to us, it would make it so much easier for us to be parents now." No, all they could do was to be faithful in the present with a faith-filled eye for the future.

Similarly, Rachel experienced in the present the blessings of those lessons from the Bible, living and breathing them daily, often playing them out with her sisters and dolls. As the present moved along one day at a time, year by year, the real-life, present-day living changed and grew along with her age and maturation. Each day Jesus was leading her along the pathway of life, she was being challenged by Him to live authentically in the present. Whether it was acknowledging the fears she faced or treasuring the joys of the day, it was in being real in the moment that Rachel became the empathetic, peace-loving person God called her to be. This is reflected in the following thoughts written by her sister-in-law, Lynette Schrader, two days after Rachel went Home:

November 8, 2012:

Jesus, My heart is sad and heavy. Our dear Rachel has gone away from us, and I am crushed to think of family times without her. Memories flood my heart:

Christmas 2007 in their home in Minnesota … The sparkle in her eyes … Her beautiful smile. She was so thrilled to have us all there. She doesn't bustle, she just calmly and gently keeps things moving. I will always remember her gentleness, her kindness.

I remember many conversations in the bedroom upstairs at the farm. I would go up to change a baby's diaper or feed a baby. Soon I'd hear a tap on the door, and Rachel would slip in for a heart-to-heart chat. I felt safe with her. Safe enough to share things with her that I have only shared with a few people. She knew me and loved and accepted and celebrated who I am and what God was doing in me. How I will miss those talks!

Rachel was also my walking partner during family reunions. At least once, we'd slip away to walk and talk. She was always willing to share her own journey and struggles with me. She was honest and authentic. Sincere. She always listened and cared. She never made me feel like a project, someone to be fixed. I knew she loved me as I was, for who I was, and I loved her back.

She does not leave just a hole in the Schrader family, she leaves a cavern. It was her gentle leadership that pulled most family reunions together. It was she who cared for Mom when health problems arose. It was she who helped keep ongoing email contact between us. Her frequent, usually short but always significant, emails blessed me. I saved most of them. She was willing to share her joys and sadnesses with us. I cried when I read her short email sharing her tears when Marcel and Carita moved to PA and Asher was soon to leave the nest too. Rachel so often provided the link that kept us connected across the miles, forwarding text messages of earthquakes in Costa Rica, flights across oceans, and other thoughts. I find myself wondering: how will we go on without her?

I remember her struggle to trust as Kristi was diagnosed with a brain tumor. How God gave her rainbows—promises of His presence and love. I remember her struggle not to give in to fear when she sensed that someone would get hurt skiing, and for trust when Asher was hurt that very day.

I remember her journey to understanding more and more of God's love for her, of watching her live more and more out of that place of being loved. Love for God and others spilled out of her. I knew it came from her relationship with Jesus.

I remember her fierce love and passion for her husband and children. How much she loved these gifts God gave her! She was a great mom and wife. How much it would hurt her to know the pain her home-going has caused her dearest ones.

I remember that Rachel loved life, and she loved us. I know she would want us to again enjoy the brilliant blue sky, the beauty of the sunset, family laughter. She would not want us to lose ourselves in sadness. She would want us to rejoice in her graduation to the fullness of Life. She would want us to trust in God's goodness. May God grant us grace to honor Rachel by seeing His goodness and grace in the midst of this darkness.

Some of us are worshippers. Some of us are servants. Some of us are teachers or writers. Rachel was a lover. A passionate lover of God, her family and friends. She truly cared. I'll never forget this. I celebrate so many things about Rachel, but mostly I remember her quiet, gentle strength and wisdom. How much I am going to miss her!

The Bride of Christ

Max Lucado once said, "A woman's heart should be so hidden in God that a man has to seek Him just to find her." No less should be said for the Bride of Christ—she should be so hidden in God that folks cannot find her unless they first find God. Seems like that should go without saying, but too many times it doesn't. In fact, sometimes the more of "church" that people see, the less they can see of God. But when Jesus is truly allowed to be the Head of the church, He stands far above everything else. And when folks see Him, they find His church there, too, worshipping at His feet.

From Jesus, people's lives move in one of two directions. On the one hand, the closer we get to Him, the closer we get to each other. But on the other hand, the more we fail to focus on Him, the farther away we will move from those who do. Jesus is the greatest uniter of people in the sense that everyone who worships Him, calls upon His name for salvation, and keeps their eyes "fixed on Jesus, the author and finisher of their faith" is drawn together around Him. But He is also the greatest divider of people in the sense that everyone who refuses to worship Him, rejects Him as Savior and Lord of their lives, and fails to make Him the focus of their faith moves in a completely opposite direction from those who do.

Jesus made all the difference in Rachel's life. And He makes all the difference in the life of the church, the Bride of Christ. The most intimate relationship is the one between the Bride of Christ and her Bridegroom. Without intimacy, there really is no relationship. A group of people may organize themselves and call themselves a church. They may rally around all kinds of good ideas and activities and outline many good doctrines to embrace, but unless they are intimately in love with Jesus their Bridegroom, they are not the Bride of Christ; they are not the church of Jesus Christ.

Reflections in Marriage

We want to observe here in these sections of each chapter, seven reflections of how our marriages are to reflect our relationship with Jesus. It's a study of how husbands and wives relating to each other is a picture of Christ and the church in relationship.

Now this is not necessarily intended to be a doctrinal thesis on marriage. Instead, it's to provide some much needed inspiration. It is intended to *inspire* marriages more than to *instruct* them. When inspiration occurs, things happen. Not that there's anything wrong with doctrine. In fact, doctrine is a very necessary thing. Doctrine provides the basic framework from which we live. Inspiration, on the other hand, provides the motivation which makes that framework come alive. That's what these sections are about. You'll find them outlined toward the end of each chapter.

Here then is the biblical context from which these seven points are inspired: Ephesians 5:21-28 (The Message):

"Out of respect for Christ, be courteously reverent to one another. Wives, understand and support your husbands in ways that show your support for Christ. The husband provides leadership to his wife the way Christ does to his church, not by domineering but by cherishing. So just as the church submits to Christ as he exercises such leadership, wives should likewise submit to their husbands.

"Husbands, go all out in your love for your wives, exactly as Christ did for the church—a love marked by giving, not getting. Christ's love makes the church whole. His words evoke her beauty. Everything he does and says is designed to bring the best out of her, dressing her in dazzling white silk, radiant with holiness. And that is how husbands ought to love their wives. They're really doing themselves a favor—since they're already "one" in marriage."

"How-Tos" For Couples

Our RELATIONSHIP: Her happiness!

So when the guys asked me, "How do I connect with my wife's heart?" and I replied, "Just make her happy," what did that look like for me? How did I make Rachel happy? Well, to begin with, for her, happiness in marriage was all about relationship, to feel personally connected and emotionally attached to me in such a way that she felt a oneness. Without a doubt, she truly loved the distinctive "me," but even more than loving me, she loved the relationship she had with me. There was her and there was me, but what good were either of us if we could not somehow marry the two?

R __elationship____ Husbands: More than she loves you, she loves this.

C _____Talk about yourself or don't bother getting married!

O _____She is body modest, but soul naked.

C _____Give her as many of these as her heart desires.

C _____Tender words, gentle touch, and a good …
F _____Share these: What's hers is yours.
F _____This comes along with the marriage.
Plus M _____The wonder of it all.

For Rachel, one rose meant as much as a dozen. She didn't really like it when I brought her a whole vase full of roses. She preferred just one. To her that one rose represented the singularity of "us." It represented the unity of our oneness, the uniqueness of me and her together, of me and her in relationship. That's what made our marriage a happy thing to her. Why corrupt its meaning with a dozen roses!

Rachel's first love language was quality time. Looking back, if there was one thing I'd change about the twenty-eight years and seventeen days of our marriage, it would be saying "no" many more times to a bunch of other people and "yes" a whole lot more to quality, solo times with her. When I focused on our relationship—that to her was quality time. And because that's where her heart was, it made her happy! And since that is what made her happy, that's exactly what I tried to do. When I relegated everything else to its proper place and focused on her, she was happy. Very, very happy!

So, how do you get in touch with your wife's heart? Just make her happy! This means putting your relationship front and center. I'm thinking your wife might be similar to mine. And I'm guessing that even more than loving you, she loves her relationship with you. If you neglect your relationship, her spirit will become matriarchal and overbearing, morphing into something more monstrous than you want. So don't neglect it. Instead, select it as your number one priority after God!

CHAPTER 3

The Bride in Adolescence

Rachel's Story

My best effigies for an adolescent Rachel are her two daughters. I didn't know Rachel until she was twenty-four years old, so I draw from her stories of growing up, as well as reports from her parents and tales from her siblings. But my best sense for who she was comes from these two images of her: Carita and Kristi. I know them. I watched them grow up, and I watched how Rachel mothered them in all the heartfelt ways she had been mothered throughout her own growing up years.

While scholars find it difficult to agree on a precise definition for adolescence, it is generally viewed as the transitional period between childhood and adulthood. One day the adolescent may feel and act like an adult and the next day he or she may feel and act like a child. This often causes much consternation for both adolescents and parents, and perhaps for others as well. *Who am I? How am I supposed to behave? What do I really enjoy? What makes me uncomfortable? Why am I so often misunderstood by others? Do I even understand myself?* Add to all this that soon after Rachel turned twelve, a sixth child was born into her family and soon after she turned fourteen, a seventh child. Being the oldest of the seven, it's an understatement to venture that Rachel even had time to know who she was. Growing up, she always felt responsible for others while at the same time feeling totally responsible for herself too. (While she could never remember sitting on her mother's lap, I do have a June 1962 black and white photo of her sitting on her Dad's lap at six years of age, along with her sister Miriam who was 16 months younger.)

In *Hope for the Family*, Dr. Marlin Howe outlines a typical family script that results from something he calls triangling. Family-system triangling begins as a relationship problem between the husband and wife. Whenever there is a lack of intimacy between the spouses, in order to compensate for that distancing, a spouse may bring in another person or thing in the family, sometimes even something outside the family. Since the perimeter of a triangle and the area inside a triangle always remain the same regardless of how the lengths of the various sides change, it is true that you cannot lengthen one side of a triangle without shortening another side. So if the distance between the husband and wife becomes greater than it should be, someone (or something) else within the family system will be drawn in closer, probably too close. With such triangulation come four possible outcomes for the children: a Hero, a Scapegoat, a Lost Child, and a Clown. The Hero, of course, is the child who never strays far from the fold, but if he or she does, they always return "bearing their sheaves with them." They are seen as heroic! The Scapegoat, as you might guess, is the child who strays unashamedly and therefore gets blamed for almost everything that's wrong in the family system. Emotionally then, they are often sent out into the wilderness to die alone. The Lost Child doesn't really know who he or she is. That's because of being so busy keeping track of everyone else and picking up after everyone else that they hardly have time for a conscious thought of themselves. Really they do have such thoughts at a subconscious level, and it erodes their sense of personal identity. Cognitively their sense of self-worth is high, because of the significant role they play, but at a heart level they feel neglected. The Clown actually feels much the same way but pacifies himself or herself by turning everything into humor. That's how they cope.

Obviously, these are sweeping generalities, but I know in looking back upon her childhood years, Rachel would most closely identify with the feelings of the Lost Child. Yet it always amazed me how she embraced this role. She never blamed anyone for it. She simply shouldered the responsibility she felt and leaned into it. And while it eroded her sense of personal confidence, she was doggedly determined to explore her relationship with the Lord in ways I have witnessed few other people willing to do. She was on a trajectory toward levels of security in Christ over the last fifteen years of her life that finally landed her perfectly safe in the arms of Jesus. She was clearly at her zenith here on earth with yet so much to offer the rest of us, we thought... and still do.

Her Inspiration

One of Rachel's best friends, her sister-in-law Lynette, says it so well, and I will simply let her say it here in something else she wrote soon after Rachel's death. I don't know if I'll ever be able to read this without the flood of tears it inevitably brings and with it a refreshing cleansing for my soul. Always.

Thoughts and recollections of Rachel Witmer, in honor of her as my friend, my sister-in-law, and my sister in Christ:

I celebrate Rachel's life, lived beautifully in service to Jesus and others. I'll never forget you, Rachel. I delight to think that you'll be there to greet me when I am called Home. You always did lead the way for me. Once again, you have done that.

Yesterday, I cried through much of the Easter worship service. The tears were two-fold. Incredible gratefulness for the cross and all Jesus accomplished for us there filled my soul. Love for my Savior, Redeemer, Lover of my Soul, washed over me. I longed to be in heaven worshipping Him for all He's done for me.

And tears came because I knew my sweet sister-in-law was there, her first Easter in heaven. Can you imagine Easter in heaven?! The celebration? The unbridled joy? The uninhibited worship? I was tasting it in my soul here on earth. She was experiencing it in the full in heaven. I longed to be there, too. The tears ran. I'm coming to realize that death is not something you get over, or recover from. It is something you come to accept and find peace with. But the missing continues. A new chapter of life has begun. It can be full of joy and Jesus, but it is new. And the missing is there.

So what are the things I miss and will keep missing about Rachel?

I'll miss our walks. I'm not sure how it came about, but it came to be a tradition that we took a nice long walk together, snow or sun, warm or cold, whenever the family was together. It was a time for our own conversation, for us to share our journeys and sorrows and joys with no other ears listening. I felt so comfortable with Rachel. She was a good listener. She asked the right questions, probing deeper into my thoughts and feelings. She validated my feelings, never minimized them. I knew I could share anything with her, and not be judged. She saw God at work in me, and she encouraged me in my journey toward Him. She truly loved and valued me. I know that because she never ever made me feel like a project she was trying to fix. Whether she agreed with where I was at or not, she accepted me and valued me as a person worth loving.

I think that is really huge for several reasons: so often we humans live manipulating and controlling each other in an attempt to get our own needs filled, and making others be what we want them to be. The fact that Rachel did not do that says something significant about her relationship with her heavenly Father. She didn't need me to be her clone in order for her to love and accept me. She didn't need me to fill her needs. She was filled. She could simply love. That is true freedom: living as a loved Child and Bearer of the Image so we can simply love others. Call them into deeper truths, but love them without strings attached. She did this more beautifully than anyone else I know.

I'll miss her friendship. On our walks, she also shared as freely as I did. She was honest. She was vulnerable. She didn't expect me to share my heart and then withhold her own. She shared things that caused her great pain. She shared things she feared and the struggle she had at times to live in trust, forgiveness, and freedom. She offered the truth of freedom to me, while at the same time honestly wrestling in her own journey toward it. She was not Miss Perfection, I've Arrived, Be Like Me. She lived the life line that author and counselor Terry Wardle uses, and which I have adopted for myself: "I am healed. I am being healed. I have yet to be healed." Rachel was an honest wrestler who fought to live free in Christ's love, while at the same time encouraging those around her to fight for their freedom in Christ as well.

I'll miss her encouragement. It was Rachel, in fact, who first encouraged me to truly fight for inner healing and freedom from fear and rejection and inner turmoil. It was Rachel who knew the places in my heart that were deeply hurt. She encouraged Tim and me to go through inner healing prayer counseling. She led the way for me as she sought her own inner healing and cheered on my pursuit. I needed far more inner healing than she did, and today, I am an amazingly different person, wonderfully healed inside, as a result of this journey. And it was Rachel who pointed the way for me.

I'll miss her gentle spirit. Perhaps what made Rachel so extraordinary was her very ordinariness. She was pretty, but not a knockout. She was successful, but not by the world's standards. She didn't go to college, or have a high-powered "job." She dressed nicely, but not all that fashionably. She was not a flashy sanguine personality. Yet, something very sweet and pure emanated from her and made her—by nature a rather quiet, reserved person—into a leader, someone all of us looked to for direction, for inspiration, for leadership. Her gentle, kind, spirit and sincere love for others were a magnet that attracted others to her. Yes, in many ways she was "ordinary." But Jesus radiating through her transformed her and made her an extraordinary and incredibly special person.

As I end these reflections, I have one more thought: To me, Rachel was the ideal woman. Strong, yet quiet. Wise. Gentle. Soft-spoken. Patient. She was an awesome mom, a supportive and submissive wife.

I have often compared myself to her, and come up short. Patience: wow, I really fall short on this one! Soft-spoken, well, let's not even talk about it! Gentleness. Hmm. I need to work on that one too. Wise. God has birthed much life in me, but I still have much to learn. Quiet. Definitely not. The list goes on in my mind. Perhaps others of you in the family feel that too. Rachel was so special, I'd like to be like her, yet I fall so short!

This is the word God has spoken to my heart. He doesn't want me or anyone else to be Rachel. There will only be one Rachel. Like all of us, she truly was indispensable. There will be only one Lynette, or Becky, or Ann Marie, or Kristi or any of us. I need to be who God made me to be. And it won't look like Rachel. It will look like Jesus in Lynette.

I think ultimately what made Rachel the incredible person that she was is that she became who God made her to be. She didn't become exactly like some other great women role models; no, she became herself: redeemed, forgiven, journeying, and sweetly walking as the person God intended her to be from her conception.

My goal needs to be the life of Jesus created in ME, not Lynette becoming like Rachel. Rachel's life will always inspire me, challenge me, encourage me to be more like Jesus. I will always think of her as the ideal. But my goal cannot be to become like her. My goal needs to be becoming like Jesus. And since I have a very different personality from Rachel, it won't look the same. But that doesn't mean it can't be good. And knowing Rachel as

I do, I know that she would be happy with this God-whispered word to my heart.

I love Rachel. I'll always miss her. In writing this, I am attempting to release her, to grasp the reality that she is gone from me, from us, for this season. I also hold close the reality that she is not gone forever. She has only gone first to our true Home, to our true Father. And so I wait in faith and hope and expectation of a glorious reunion.

Rachel with her brother Tim and Lynette at
Marcel and Krista's wedding reception.

The Bride of Christ

The church is a place to call home. It's the place where we belong. It's the place we are born into through no fault of our own, but by love offered and love received. The church is the place where we learn to walk and to talk, where we can fall down and have others help us get back up on our feet, where we can find our voice and learn to enunciate life. The church is a place of brothers and sisters—older siblings and younger ones too; a father and mother: a sovereign, all powerful God and a compassionate, relational Savior. The church is the place where the Comforter lives and guides us by His peace toward everything right.

The church is a place for adolescents—that transitional place between where we had been and where we are going. That place where we're so heavenly minded we seem no earthly good in the natural, yet so earthly minded many times we're no heavenly good to the Spirit. But we are safe. And though we sometimes wonder who we are in this place, we have the assurance we can stay; and although we are not fully mature, we know we are well on the way.

Reflections in Marriage

What is the meaning of marriage? What did God have in mind when He took Adam's rib and created Eve around it, bringing them together in marriage? What did Adam mean when he said, "This is now bone of my bone and flesh of my flesh; she shall be called woman." Exactly what is it in a man that makes a woman? And what is it in their union that makes a marriage?

We don't get very far into the New Testament theology of marriage until we come across Ephesians 5, which outlines for us in colorful detail God's design for marriage. He stages it as a picture, a symbol of something greater, or as we're considering it here, a reflection. Now if you have a reflection of something, there has to be something else that is being reflected. There is something *real* on the one hand that is showing up as a *reflection* on the other hand. For example, consider Rainy Lake in northern Minnesota on a calm summer day, the peaceful stillness of the water reflecting perfectly the beautiful scenery along the shore, so much so that you can hardly tell which are the actual flowers and trees along the shoreline and which are merely reflections of those flowers and trees.

Similarly in Scripture we discover that marriage is a reflection … an ordinance, to use the proper ecclesiastical jargon. An ordinance is an earthly sign with a heavenly meaning, or to say it another way, a physical symbol with spiritual significance. In other words, it is something on this earth that is intended to be a picture of something in heaven; something within this earthly framework illustrating something in the spiritual realm. Marriage is a type. It is the shadow of something much larger and more real than itself. And remember, shadows are always true to their substance! A reflection is always congruent to the real thing it is reflecting.

Now this may at first seem a little disappointing to those who are married to think that marriage is not an end in itself. I'm sorry, but that's all it is—just an earthly illustration. It is not the real thing in terms of heaven and eternity. The real thing is Jesus Christ and the relationship He wants to have with His people. Our marriages are pictures of that relationship. Now that's significant, isn't it? So maybe it's not so disappointing after all!

"How-Tos" For Couples

Our CONNECTION: Her Happiness!

Let me talk about how connection brought happiness to Rachel. It was so close to her heart! I highly suspect it's the same for your wife, the mother of your kids.

R __elationship____ Husbands: More than she loves you, she loves this.
C __onnection____ Talk about yourself or don't bother getting married!
O _____ She is body modest, but soul naked.
C _____ Give her as many of these as her heart desires.
C _____ Tender words, gentle touch, and a good …
F _____ Share these: What's hers is yours.
F _____ This comes along with the marriage.
Plus M _____ The wonder of it all.

Connection is obviously related to relationship but more specific. A synonym might be the word "togetherness." Rachel did not want a disconnected relationship, but one bonded by our common connectors. There were particular connecting points that drew us toward each other in the first place and that kept us together for over twenty-eight years. We discovered these connectors through self-disclosure—a critical piece to marriage. To all want-to-be husbands: If you're not willing to talk about yourself, don't bother getting married! All through our marriage, when Rachel was able to feel those connections, it made her very happy! Being a woman, her sense of connection was primarily built around her heart, but she also wanted spiritual, physical, and intellectual connections.

Our greatest connection in marriage was around our common faith in Christ. She loved it when we prayed and studied Scripture together, not just in a ritualistic, formal way but especially in an "around-the-supper-table" or "hiking-around-the-block" sort of way where it would just kind of seep into our experience without fanfare. She loved the same experiences with our children as a family all together. And, of course, this was also our greatest connection in terms of ministry. One of our last significant ministry connections was leading a 91-year-old man to Christ as we stood around his hospital bed. Also, four days before her death, we stopped in to deliver $500 to a local family with whom we'd been doing a bilingual Bible study. These were spiritual experiences we had together that connected deeply with her.

Even as a woman, she loved physical connection. She liked being together in the same room rather than at opposite ends of the house. She loved sitting close to me on the couch; I remember wounding her spirit one time when I wiggled around for more space. She loved it when I took her hand and looked her in the eye, or when I simply held her hand in prayer. Or, just like she loved God's hugs when He gave her rainbows to see, she loved it when I'd hug her too. And while she didn't often initiate our sexual connections, she welcomed and enjoyed them, comparing them to our intimacy with Christ in passages of Scripture like, "Christ in you, the hope of glory," and like the golden lampstand in the book of Revelation where it says Christ is seen "in the midst of" His people, fulfilling His purposes in them. Rachel appreciated the fact that marriage typified Christ's connections with His Bride, the church.

Intellectual connections were also important to her. Most significant here was probably our agreement around children— how they should be enthusiastically welcomed into our family, but that our family should not be a child-CENTERED home. Child-connected? Yes! Child-centered? No. So it goes without saying, we agreed on child training. We also had a common understanding about the kind of lifestyle we should lead, what kind of neighborhood we should live in, and how to interact within that community. We also had similar intellectual views about more marginal things like politics. So, while the meeting of the minds was not our first priority, it was a connecting point that mattered to her.

Heart connection and spirit connection, physical connection and intellectual connection—in that order—this was Rachel, my wife and the mother of our kids. She lived by connection. No wonder it hurt so much when she needed to leave!

CHAPTER 4

Age of Accountability

Rachel's Story

Rachel grew up in the Freeport Mennonite Church where her great-grandfather Simon Graybill was a minister back in the early 1900s and where her brother Dave is currently the pastor. She was very familiar with the church and of church-life there, and it was not without knowledge of the ministry and pastoral care that she took on the role of a pastor's wife when I was ordained at Northwood Chapel in Minnesota on June 2, 1990. Rachel was baptized July 7, 1969, at thirteen years of age. A major influence in her life during that time was her Sunday school teacher Dorothy Shelly. Rachel spoke highly of Dorothy and of the influence she had in her life during those years. Each Sunday at the end of her class-time, Dorothy would rehearse the plan of salvation and encourage her students to accept Christ into their hearts.

On the Sunday of Rachel's conversion, the pastor gave a special invitation at the end of his message for anyone wanting to accept Christ to stand to their feet. Rachel stood and recalls how her Dad put his arm around her. Later they prayed together when she asked Jesus to come into her heart and make her into a new person, born-again by the power of the Holy Spirit. From that day on, her life took on a whole new direction and purpose.

Her Inspiration

Rachel had a way of keeping everyone in her family encouraged along the way. Here's something she emailed to the entire Schrader family on March 12, 2012, eight months before her death. It was an excerpt from Joni Eareckson Tada's book, *A Place of Healing*.

Jack Reimer, a syndicated columnist, wrote a story about the great violinist Yitzhak Perlman. Perlman had polio as a child and walks with crutches and braces on both legs. Instead of arranging to be seated on stage at the beginning of his performance, he chooses to walk across the stage methodically and slowly until he reaches his chair. Then he sits down, puts his crutches on the floor, undoes the clasps on his legs, bends down, picks up the violin, nods to the conductor, and proceeds to play. As Reimer describes it, there is a certain majesty in this ritual.

During a 1995 concert, a string on Perlman's violin suddenly snapped, and everyone in the audience could hear it. The great virtuoso stopped and gazed at the broken string as those in attendance that night wondered what he would do. Perlman closed his eyes, and after a moment of reflection, signaled the conductor to begin again.

Though anyone who knows music understands that it's impossible to play a symphonic work with just three strings, Perlman was undaunted. Apparently you could see this superb artist actually recomposing the piece in his head as he went along, inventing new fingering positions to coax never-before-heard sounds from his three-string violin.

The sophisticated New York audience watched and listened in awe, knowing they were witnessing a truly groundbreaking performance. When the piece was over, they exploded into appreciative applause. Mr. Perlman smiled, wiped the sweat from his brow, and said in a soft, reverent tone, "You know, sometimes it is the artist's task to find out how much music you can still make with what you have left."

That's another truth that enables me to keep going. Whatever strings are broken in our lives, if we concentrate, if we apply what we know, we can still play beautiful music with what we have left. In fact, it will be music that no one else can play in the same way.

The Bride of Christ

Just like children coming to the age of accountability in taking personal responsibility for their sins, there must be a sense of personal responsibility within the corporate body of the church in giving account for who we are, what we believe, and how we behave. We must continue nurturing that sense of personal responsibility within the church at this level. The "age of accountability" must come for all of us within the church if we are to develop mature, reproducing churches within our culture. After all, that's what it's like for children growing up. They are used to their parents dictating moral norms for them and telling them what's right and wrong, but there comes a day when they must come to terms with their own consciences and take responsibility for their attitudes and actions. Within the church body, too many of us are used to letting the church dictate to us what we should believe and how we should behave. But the day has come when we must own for ourselves what we believe and why. And I tell you, when the church body—the Bride of Christ—embraces that level of accountability, she will have moved into a whole new level of belief, behavior, beauty, and effectiveness in both evangelism and discipleship.

Someone has said, "Accountability is like the right-of-way at an intersection of roadways; it's something you give, not take." It can be a bit frightening at both of these intersections: the age of accountability for children and the age of accountability for churches. Whereas the unmerited grace and mercy of God keeps children safe before the age of accountability and releases them afterwards to the work of the Holy Spirit in their lives, so churches must not hover over their members in ways that measure out every application of God's Word for them, play God in their consciences, and insist on everyone thinking and practicing just like everyone else. It's a demonic fear that keeps parents from allowing the Holy Spirit free access to their children, and it's even more so for churches to forbid their members from having their own relationship of accountability before God. Every generation must personally grapple with and apply principles of truth in their day.

With this in mind, I recall a slice of Scripture strategically located in 1 Corinthians 11, right after the teaching about the headship veiling and communion that I've come to call the most "heretical" verse in the Bible.

The Most "Heretical" Verse in the Bible

After completing over sixty percent of his first letter to the Corinthians in an effort to correct heresy in the church, it sounds like the inspired biblical writer, Paul, doubles back on himself and suggests that the tension of heresy is a necessary ingredient. Is that what he really means? Let's find out.

Three questions we should ask ourselves whenever we bump into a Scripture we don't understand are: 1) What does it actually say? 2) What does it mean? and 3) What does it mean to us today? Let's consider the most important one first.

I.   **WHAT DOES IT ACTUALLY SAY?** Here is 1 Corinthians 11:19 in three commonly respected versions:

KJV	NASB	NIV
19 For there must be also heresies among you, that they which are approved may be made manifest among you.	**19** For there must also be factions among you, in order that those who are approved may become evident among you.	**19** No doubt there have to be differences among you to show which of you have God's approval.

In the vernacular of Scripture, there it is. But what does it say in everyday English? The NASB and the NIV, more recent translations, are a little easier to understand, but even then we are still left wondering a bit. Three words in this verse need to be defined if we are going to know what it says. We need to understand what "heresy" means, what "approved" means, and what "manifest" means. Let's look at the Greek dictionary definitions since this verse was first written in Greek.

A) **DEFINITION OF "HERESY."**
   1. <u>Heresy</u> = A choice, a party, disunion, heresy
   2. <u>Heresy</u> = Half-truth, truth taken in isolation, truth sundered from counter-truth.

3. <u>Heresy</u> = Self-willed opinion which is substituted for submission to the <u>power of truth</u>; such opinions are frequently the outcome of <u>personal preference</u> or the prospect of <u>advantage</u>.

4. Heresies = dissensions arising from a diversity of opinions and aims.

B) DEFINITION OF "APPROVAL."

1. <u>Approved</u> = Acceptable, tried
   "when he is <u>tried</u>, he shall come forth as gold" James 1:12.

2. <u>Approved</u> = Approved of God
   "Salute Apelles <u>approved</u> in <u>Christ</u>. Salute them which are of Aristobulus' household" Rom. 16:10.
   "For not he that commendeth himself <u>is</u> <u>approved</u>, but <u>whom the Lord</u> commendeth" 2 Cor. 10:18.
   "Study to show thyself <u>approved</u> <u>unto</u> <u>God</u> … rightly dividing the word of truth" 2 Tim. 2:15.

C) DEFINITION OF "MANIFEST"

1. <u>Manifest</u> = shining, apparent, public, external, open (Strong's)
2. <u>Manifest</u> = open to sight, visible, shining (Vine's)

II. WHAT DOES IT MEAN?

Now that we got through the heavy task of determining what this verse actually *says*, let's figure out what it *means*. Unless we know what is meant, it doesn't do us much good. In order to discover what is meant, we must look at the context in which it was written. We make seven discoveries when looking at it contextually:

1) **They were coming together only to be divided.** The Corinthian Christians might as well have stayed home and done their own thing if they were going to come together only to divide up and hold each other at arm's length, highlighting their differences.

   In our zeal for doctrinal purity, we as conservative Christians often spend more time emphasizing what we're against than what we're *for*! But nothing can be more doctrinally pure than keeping our focus right, as we discussed in Chapter 2: "Jesus Christ and Him crucified." Yet we so often end up emphasizing everything but that.

Rather than rally around WHO we have in common, we strut up our differences. Not that it's never right to discuss and even debate doctrinal issues and how they matter in practical life, but if in so doing, we self-congratulate ourselves and belittle others, we have surely aligned ourselves with the Pharisees and not with Jesus.

2) **They were self-indulgent.** Each one did what felt good to himself and his own clique, rather than controlling himself for the benefit of others. Self-denial and deference to others seems to be a lost art among American believers in every denomination. Deference to the "weaker brother" is a mark of spiritual maturity but must not be confused with capitulating to the carnal. The weaker brother is someone whose salvation or sanctification is at stake. A carnal person is someone who simply needs to have things his or her way to be happy. We are doing no one a favor if we accommodate carnality or even immaturity. Paul challenged the believers that instead of being able to eat meat, they were still only surviving on milk. But at the same time we must be careful not to jeopardize someone's walk with the Lord.

3) **The poor (the vulnerable) were neglected.** Not only were the widows neglected, but anyone who was spiritually vulnerable was also going to be neglected by such distractions. I well remember the utter grief we experienced in a previous church setting when the pros and cons of facial hair was made an issue for a newborn Christian who was reeling from his recent divorce and struggling to maintain good connections with his little son and two daughters. Needless to say, his spiritual vitals soon registered code blue.

Even now in my early fifties, having walked with the Lord for forty years and pastored churches for nearly twenty-five, I have felt a deep panic of spirit in the midst of grieving the loss of my wife when good brothers and sisters want to major on minors while I'm just trying to make it through the day. I don't believe we can emphasize enough the absolute imperative of focusing on "Jesus, the author and finisher of our faith" rather than fixating on each other and nit-picking our petty differences.

4) **The way they were doing things was not good—better off not to do it at all (v. 17).** Paul essentially declares here that it would have been better to do nothing than to do the <u>right</u>

thing in the <u>wrong</u> way. Of course, the best would have been to do the <u>right</u> thing the <u>right</u> way. Recently when teaching the principles of headship from verses 1–16 of this chapter, I declared that it would be better not to practice the headship veiling at all than to be making an external show of something that was not in fact true in spirit and behavior. It's better for a husband and wife to be functioning together in mutual love and respect but missing the value of symbolism in the headship veiling than to be doggedly practicing the symbol but missing the real substance of how headship is lived out in their lives.

In Luke 12:1, Jesus called hypocrisy the leaven of the Pharisees. And in Matthew 23, He seems to have finally gotten His fill of their stuff and just lays it out to them straight with a stunning, seven-point lecture of "woes." "Woe unto you scribes and Pharisees—hypocrites!" Bam, bam, bam. Seven times He hits them right between the eyes about their make-believe religiosity.

5) **That "heresies" (issues) reveal the heart condition.** Heresies, or factions or differences, usually do more to reveal the true heart condition of people than anything else. This is why the Apostle Paul says, "It must needs be." There is real value in the tensions heresies produce. They tend to demonstrate what we're really made of. I have sometimes failed this test. But always, whether I'm approved or disproven, I'm reminded of how essential such testing is. I miss Rachel's ability to check my spirit under tension. She always believed in me and constantly looked to me for leadership in tricky situations, but at the same time was able to qualify my spirit in the process. It was a mutual benefit we both were able to experience at critical times with each other.

6) **There are always those who are approved by God.** In spite of all the tomfoolery that can go on in the name of truth, holiness, pure doctrine, or proper performance, there is always a remnant of people who can keep focused no matter what. Praise God! "Jesus Christ and Him crucified" must be our single eye.

A couple of years ago Rachel and I were flying with our two youngest to Rachel's parents in Illinois for Thanksgiving. In the Minneapolis airport on a short layover, there was this restless, shifty-eyed fellow who kept fumbling around with his boarding pass, dropping it on the floor, picking it up again, and then sitting down on one of the seats in the waiting area, standing up again, walking around a bit more, dropping his pass again, glancing around at others, heading off down the concourse at a rapid pace, then abruptly turning around and heading back again. It was obvious this fellow was agitated, worried, and paranoid about what he was supposed to be doing and where he was supposed to be going. Different ones of us tried to talk to him and help him, but he shook us off and went his own way again. Eventually we all boarded, and the man got to his seat. When we landed in Chicago, there were family members waiting for him who immediately took him under their wings and all was well.

Some Christians and some churches remind me of this fellow. They're agitated, worried about their surroundings, and paranoid of other people. They give lip service to the fact that they trust Jesus as the pilot, have obviously chosen His airline, and claim to have their destiny in view. But they cannot focus upon Christ, keep getting distracted by fears, and suspect everyone else is out to take advantage of them somehow. But, praise the Lord, for every insecure believer, there are others who are secure in Christ, able to stay focused, and can rest in the approval of God.

7) **Those who are approved will always be made known.** It should come as no surprise that those who honor God, God will honor. They don't have to go around tooting their own horn or booing those who oppose them. All they have to do is "study to be approved unto God," and He will make His approval obvious. This doesn't mean they'll never be challenged or even attacked by those who feel threatened. We live in a fallen world and our churches absorb some of the fallout, but in the end, "faithful is He who has called you, who also will do it" (1 Thess. 5:23–24). God is able to complete that which He has begun.

I've lived long enough and experienced enough flak in life to have seen how the test of time can prove the faithfulness of God. Anymore I consider it a badge of honor to be singled out for opposition. Every man of God whom I respect has been targeted in the same ways and many times by the same opponents. I'm humbled that God has counted me worthy to partake in the sufferings of Christ. If I follow His example and trace His footsteps through the maze of life's confusing twists and turns, someday I will hear His welcome voice saying, "Enter thou into the joy of thy Lord."

III. WHAT DOES IT MEAN TO US?

So, what does this all mean <u>for us</u>?

1) **We must be careful about driving wedges and highlighting differences.** Where we stand in relation to each other is very, very secondary. The real question is where we stand in relation to God. So why bother to highlight how I stand apart from someone else, unless I'm insecure and like to drive wedges?

2) **We must beware of carnal motivations (self-willed opinions).** Most wedges that people use to divide are simply that: self-willed opinions. When motivations are pure from the heart, most differences—within the context of Scripture—don't even matter.

3) **In Christ we are all one—equal, with no differences.** No true unity is ever possible without an exclusive focus upon Christ. Everything within the peripheral scope of things must contribute to a Christ-centered focus. If it does not, it is merely a distraction and will cause cross-sightedness, confusion, and division.

4) **Remember that just because "this is the way it's always been" doesn't make it right.** If "the way it has always been" is wrong, it will be wrong no matter how long it has been that way. In fact, the longer it is that way, the more wrong it is! Every generation must personally grapple with and apply principles of truth in their day.

5) **We must check our hearts! What is driving us?** Are we craving personal significance and security? Or are we submitted to the "power of truth," the Greek definition for which "heresy" is the opposite? Or, is that submission to the power of truth being substituted by "self-willed opinion?"

6) **Be approved unto God!** When God approves, it doesn't matter who disapproves. And, interestingly enough, plenty of approval will come from those who have been approved by God too. And those who are not approved by God will never approve of those who are. So, why worry about them? Look for God's approval.

7) **Know that the truth will stand.** It may not always be recognized or appreciated by men, but it will stand. And you don't have to make it stand—it just will, because it's truth!

So, will the real heretics please stand up? They never do. But those who are approved by God will be made manifest. God, help us all to rest in His approval!

Reflections in Marriage

1. The Divine Proposal (Bridegroom)

THE REAL THING:
Christ, who is reflected in us as husbands, establishes His church. It's not the other way around! "I will build my church," Jesus said (Mt. 16:18). "For other foundation can no man lay than that is laid, which is Jesus Christ" (1 Cor. 3:11). "Jesus Christ himself being the chief cornerstone" (Eph. 2:20b). It wasn't just anybody's idea. It was God's idea, and for Christ it was a no-brainer! He would build her up.

THE REFLECTION:
Man establishes his bride when he marries her. Before you groan too loud in objection, remember who the husband represents – Christ. And the wife represents the church. Does the church establish Christ? No! Not without heretical distortion. It's the other way around. The husband gives new meaning and purpose to her existence. Various cultures have various traditions, but this truth is symbolized within our culture when the bridegroom gives his bride a new name. Ever wonder where this tradition came from? Here it is:
". . . this is now bone of my bones, and flesh of my flesh: she shall be called Woman, because she was taken out of man" (Gen. 2:23).
Adam then gives additional meaning to this woman by giving her another, more personal name. "And Adam called his wife's name Eve; because she was the mother of all living" (Gen.3:20).

"How-Tos" For Couples

Our OPENNESS: Her Happiness!

Dr. Marlin Howe in *Hope for the Family* says men are body-naked but soul-modest while women are body-modest and soul-naked. That's why men's dormitory shower rooms are wide open affairs with simple shower heads poking out of the walls and no curtains in sight, but women's showers are all cordoned off with individual curtains. On the other hand, women can sit around tipsy little tables at Starbucks sipping coffee and giving each other wide open views of their souls, but if you ask a man to bare his soul, he's embarrassed and clams up.

R __elationship_____ Husbands: More than she loves you, she loves this.
C __onnection_____ Talk about yourself or don't bother getting married!
O __penness_____ She is body modest, but soul naked.
C _____ Give her as many of these as her heart desires.
C _____ Tender words, gentle touch, and a good …
F _____ Share these: What's hers is yours.
F _____ This comes along with the marriage.
Plus M _____ The wonder of it all.

Rachel was the most curious person I ever knew. She had a craving to know even the most mundane details of my life; she wanted to know my innermost thoughts and feelings on just about everything. When I shared transparently with her in this way, it caused her to feel emotionally close to me. This made her happy! And she didn't just want to know the simple facts; she wanted to know every supporting detail as well. Unless I took notes throughout my day, it would sometimes take several hours for me to remember, rewind, and report every newsworthy item to her.

So, for me to be on the same page with Rachel emotionally, I needed to be open. Actually, our personalities were a bit unusual in this regard, because even though she was a woman, she tended to be more reserved than many women, and though I'm a man, I was more transparent than most men. This worked well for us most of the time, but there were times her curiosity got the best of me, and my insensitivity made her feel closed out of my life.

I still remember in the first year of our marriage when I stonewalled on what I thought were too many questions, and she hit the dining room table with her fist in frustration. I burst out laughing; I hadn't known she had it in her to be so emphatic. It was an early marriage lesson that my wife's curiosity was not borne out of nosiness at all, but from an honest desire to truly know me from the inside out, so I best be open!

Some brides are transparently self-focused with self-infatuation. These are the conditions by which they date their men and their weddings reflect the same. It's all about them. They call it a Christian wedding because they're marrying a Christian man, their wedding occurs in a Christian church, and they may even be Christian themselves, but they set the agenda, they stage the order of events, and they are firmly centered as the focal point of the entire affair. With diaphanous wedding gowns, they may put forward a show of openness, but it's not the real thing because real women are body-modest.

Rachel was different. And I see other women today whose hearts are truly fixed on Christ and do their best to keep Him as their center point of reference. True openness of heart and mind spelled a delightful innocence for Rachel that could not be faked. It just *was*! Not only then was she happy, but happy also was the man who found her.

CHAPTER 5

The Teen Bride

Rachel's Story

One of the most beautiful photos I have of Rachel is her as a seventeen-year-old junior in high school. All the charming features of that stage in life frame her face: brunette hair in braids, slightly crooked smile, brilliantly white teeth, dark brown penetrating eyes, and slanted glasses that were in style back then in the early seventies. She'd be amused to know her daughter's college classmates are wearing that same style of glasses this year and are urging Kristi to dig out her mom's old frames to outfit her own prescription and be in style.

Speaking of seventeen years of age, Dr. Marlin Howe has identified the years 17 to 21 as a second chance parents have with their children. Most parents feel that if they've failed with their kids by the time they're teenagers, it's a lost cause, but that's simply not true for a number of reasons. To begin with, what parent doesn't feel like a failure somewhere between diapers and drivers' licenses? Secondly, Howe says that much of what kids are in temperament, outlook, and habit is not fully internalized until sometime around that 17 to 21 age. (Perhaps that's why in yesteryear, 21 was the accepted year for coming of age.) So if we as parents have not won the hearts of our children earlier on, there's a second chance! If we humble ourselves, are honest with our kids about our issues, and truly seek further purging and development in our own lives, then there's a wide open door to reconnect with the hearts of our kids in those later teenage years. But if we can't muster the transparency and humility to do so, then all bets are off.

Of course, ultimately, our children have to take personal responsibility as well. Even without spiritually minded parents, teenagers can still access the grace of God in their lives. His power can overcome any of the negative inner-developmental forces at work from their upbringing, even though the odds are stacked against them. Teenagers must be reminded not to put too much stock in their emotions. Instead, they need to trust God's divine enablement (grace) to "behave" their way into new feelings rather than trying to "feel" their way into new actions.

As a typical teenager, those years for Rachel came with a slight of temptation unfamiliar to her. In candid discussions with her girls over the years, she's recounted how peer pressure as a teenager in school led her to roll up her dresses at the waist to make them shorter. It was something she wouldn't have been allowed to leave home with, but at least she could fit into the styles at school at bit better when arriving there. Another distraction to her in those years was a guy she dated some but broke up with after he insisted she let him kiss her. What was that all about? She would never know. Of course, that was quite innocent compared to the compromises of other couples, but she felt violated by him nonetheless. And yes, there was this other poor fellow who slashed his wrists after she turned him down for a date. The issues then were small compared to the explicit environments and raw violence plaguing public schools today, but for her they were real and provided a powerful preliminary for dialogue with her daughters many years later.

These were some of the vulnerabilities Rachel experienced as a teen, but there were many assets to her in those years as well. One of the best things Rachel's parents did for her was to take her family on extended road trips, visiting friends and relatives in Indiana, Iowa, Pennsylvania, and eventually to Minnesota and on up into northern Ontario. It was on one of those trips north that their Suburban broke down on a Saturday afternoon near Grove City, Minnesota, just west of Minneapolis. As Providence would have it, they were not far from the Helmuths, a hospitable Beachy Amish family, where they were able to find space to park the little travel trailer they were camping in. They spent the weekend learning to know a whole new set of folks they would never have met otherwise.

We tend to shrug our shoulders at random circumstances, but this delay altered plans for the Schrader family in ways that shaped the rest of their lives. It ultimately steered them north through Minnesota to Blackduck, a Mennonite resort community recommended by the people from Grove City. The next Sunday morning found all seven of the Schrader children—Rachel, Miriam, Becky, Ruthanna, Dan, Dave, and Tim—all lined up alongside their parents on the front pew of the Kitchi Pines Mennonite church, which was romantically situated along the Scenic Highway halfway between Blackduck and Cass Lake. I've heard the story repeated so many times over the years about what a spectacle it was to have this large visiting family, complete with four gorgeous girls and three becoming brothers, file into church just as church was starting. Everyone in church was turning around in their seats to see if this long queue of stunning siblings would ever come to an end. Suffice it to say, this is where Miriam found her first husband, Clovis Byler, and twelve years after that, not far from Kitchi, her second husband Lester. But most exciting to me, eleven years after that triumphal entry into Kitchi, this is where I found Rachel. But that's a story for chapter nine.

Her Inspiration

Rachel's teenage years provided the background she would draw from in walking with her own children through that phase of life. She always chose to identify with them in their unique struggles, to be responsive rather than reactive, and to seek rapport in building relationships with them without the need to prove her point. This won the hearts of everyone, but certainly so with her teenagers. Some of this shines through an email addressed to her parents and siblings called, "There he goes." Rachel wrote the following:

> Carita expressed our sentiments so well: "And he's off … Marcel Witmer, the first of us Witmer children to leave home for good. He's off to marry a wonderful woman, Krista Beiler, and start life with her. It's interesting how one can feel joy and sorrow, gain and loss over the same circumstance. God is GOOD!"
>
> Do you mind if I am a bit sentimental? I didn't know it would be so hard. It hit me a while ago that as they leave for good, it is the end of an era for me. Then Krista came and they packed up his room before the two weeks of Evening Bible Camps and it hit me again—he is leaving for good this time. Didn't really have time to process that with 30 to 40 extra people around. Today I can cry.
>
> This summer he and his brothers did the Mt. Whitney hike and other last things. Last week Marcel and his best buddies (Benji Mast and Michael Yoder) took a trip to Mexico, and this week they are traveling to their eastern destinations together via Grand Canyon and Rocky Mountain National Park and it hit me that along with our children go their friends who have come to mean a lot to us as well. But it is all good, and we rejoice in the choices they have made and their desire to follow God.

Meanwhile, I hear Kristi practicing wedding music and there is sewing to do ... we are excited ... a trip to BMA convention and DNI retreat this weekend.

Quote of the day: (As we stood in front of the house, Marcel and Asher were facing each other.)

Asher: "Wow! Two months from today you ..."

Marcel with a grin on his face: "I won't be looking at you!"

Ahh! How we will miss their banter back and forth. In a month we do it all over again as Carita leaves.

I love you all,
Rachel

2010 Prayer Card photo, taken from above the Dodger Stadium.

The Bride of Christ

There are seven primary relationships all of us should have in order to experience God's full design for us. Within these relationships is a divine flow of grace enabling us not only to receive the life of His Spirit in us, but also to be life-giving channels of grace to others. These life-giving relationships are rooted in eternity but must be built from the ground up, gaining broader and broader impact, in turn providing a funnel of relationships flowing back to God.

Relationship #1: Jesus
Result: Salvation

The first relationship that matters is the one we have with Jesus. It's the most basic relationship possible for people. Jesus is a real Person! Furthermore, He now dwells in heaven where He is preparing a fantastic place for us to come and live for all eternity. Yet in spite of that ethereal, beyond our wildest imagination fact, He also knows what it's like to live here on earth—to experience fatigue, disappointment, emotional and physical pain, and every other human experience possible in this present evil world. So, even though Jesus is God, He's also human and acquainted with all our ways; He was tempted in the very same ways we are.

The Divine Flow of Life-Giving Relationships
(John 7:37-39)

UNIVERSAL CHURCH — Completion
CHURCH COMMUNITY — Momentum
LOCAL CHURCH — Interdependence
FRIENDSHIPS — Function
FAMILY — Wisdom
SELF — Sanctification

J
E
S
U
S
Salvation

Eternity

Life-giving relationships are rooted in eternity, and must be built from the-ground-up, gaining broader and broader impact, and in turn providing a funnel of relationships flowing back to God.

To have this relationship with Jesus results in our <u>salvation</u>. This relationship is so critical, because in order for us to be life-giving people, we ourselves must have His LIFE. We must be born again in a way that supersedes our natural birth. We must be spiritually reborn into a living relationship with Jesus Christ. When Jesus was here on earth, He said, "I am the good shepherd, and know my sheep, and am known of mine" (John 10:14). It's heartwarming to be called a sheep because of how peaceful and compliant sheep are, but it's especially heartwarming when you know that our Shepherd is Jesus. It's a win-win relationship! It's also encouraging to realize that Jesus *knows* us. We are not just a number on His rolodex, but He knows us personally, and because of this He wants us to really know Him too.

In verse 15, Jesus goes on to say, "As the Father knoweth me, even so know I the Father: and I lay down my life for the sheep." Jesus has connections. Big connections! He knows God, and God knows Him. No wonder, because Jesus actually *is* God. But what's really astounding is that this great God-Son with firsthand connections with God the Father also wants connection with us! And in order to have that, He gave up His life for us, the sheep. He died for us. He died for us so that we wouldn't have to die for our sins that separate us from Him. So, rather than us dying, He died! I don't know about you, but that's the kind of relationship that blows me away. Where the One who had no faults of His own took upon Himself all of my sin just so He could clear up the relationship between us.

Relationship #2: <u>Self</u>
Result: Sanctification

Having a healthy relationship first with Jesus but then also with ourselves results in our personal sanctification. The Apostle Paul says in 1 Thessalonians 5:23, "And the very God of peace sanctify you wholly; and I pray God your whole spirit and soul and body be preserved blameless unto the coming of our Lord Jesus Christ." The **second** relationship each of us has is the one with ourselves. Many people don't think about that— that they actually have a relationship with themselves. But when you stop and think about it, every human being knows the war that can sometimes develop between our spirits, our souls (mind, will, emotions), and our bodies. When we enter into that first relationship with Christ, our spirits becomes new creations, but the soul and physical parts of us are still just as they were before conversion. That is why Christian growth requires settling inner conflicts within ourselves, before we can properly relate to other people and safely minister to them.

The reason the Bible lists qualifications for elders is because it takes emotionally healthy and spiritually qualified people to maintain credibility in the hearts and minds of those they are to lead. Personal sanctification validates God's message through us. Therefore, if we attempt to relate to others—and especially if we try to help others—without first internalizing His life in sanctification, we can horribly embarrass and harm the Body of Christ which is to be His beautiful Bride.

Relationship #3: Family
Result: Wisdom

Every relational dynamic we need for life and life-giving ministry can be developed within the school of the home. Family dynamics are the **third** kind of relationship we all need, because these dynamics provide wisdom for successful living and for functioning in healthy, life-giving ministry to others. The elder Paul told the younger Timothy that a Christian bishop should be, "one that ruleth well his own house, having his children in subjection with all gravity; (For if a man know not how to rule his own house, how shall he take care of the church of God?" (1 Tim. 3:4,5).

Rachel and I have five children. Before our children came along, I thought the role of parents was to help their children grow up. I have discovered that this is only partially true. I now know that the role of children requires their parents to grow up too. You can't be selfish and successfully raise children. Children teach us how to live for others and how to relate to various ages. Babies don't care about income, titles, or influence. They demand our attention and care. If we withhold it, they'll punish us.

Relationship #4: Friendships
Result: Function

"Iron sharpeneth iron; so a man sharpeneth the countenance of his friend" (Prov. 27:17).

Every successful family, fraternity, or fellowship facilitates the formation of dynamic, life-giving friendships within that body. Friendships are the **fourth** kind of relationship we all need. They are especially significant to teenagers. Every human being longs to belong, and burning deep within the bosom of every young man or woman is the question, "Am I in?"

If they feel secure with the answer to that question, they learn how to function in life.

Friendships within the Body of Christ are especially important for they are what hold a fellowship together. Any demon, no matter how weak, can penetrate a corporate structure. But no demon, no matter how strong, can penetrate a genuine friendship. Strong healthy friendships make all of us more secure, positive, productive, and effective than we could ever be alone. They produce an upward synergy that activates strength.

Individual friendships, as well as small groups of friends, teach us how to function in the calling God has given us. In this way, the righteousness God is working into our lives is refined in a practical way. In small church groups, we learn how to apply the lessons we have learned in our personal relationship with Christ and our family relationships. Honest friendships keep us from being deceived or deluded into hypocrisy.

Relationship #5: <u>Church</u>
Result: Interdependence

> "And he gave some, apostles; and some, prophets; and some, evangelists; and some, pastors and teachers; For the perfecting of the saints, for the work of the ministry, for the edifying of the body of Christ: Till we all come in the unity of the faith, and of the knowledge of the Son of God, unto a perfect man, unto the measure of the stature of the fullness of Christ: From whom the whole body fitly joined together and compacted by that which every joint supplieth, according to the effectual working in the measure of every part, maketh increase of the body unto the edifying of itself in love" (Eph. 4:11, 13-14, 16).

Local fellowships are God's storehouses of dynamic power. When we truly tap into that resource, the result is that we begin to function in the strength of <u>interdependence</u>. It's an inside-out thing, not the other way around. Of course, we all grow as we go. But interdependent strength is exactly that — "inter," not "outer." It comes from within and cannot be merely framed or reinforced by external structure. Facades and facsimiles can, but they are not the real thing. Authentic interdependence is born from original hearts aligned in unity. In 1 Corinthians 12, the Bible reminds us that we are a Body with many members, which only function efficiently when working together. By worshiping, giving, learning, and growing together as a local body, our cumulative impact dramatically increases. Unified prayer, financial strength, and mutual encouragement cause us to form a local body of Christians capable of accomplishing tasks that would be impossible otherwise.

Ephesians 4:16 emphasizes the role of interdependent relationships within the local fellowship when it talks about the Body being "fitly joined together and compacted by that which every joint supplieth." Those supporting ligaments are the healthy relationships within the Body that cause it to grow, build itself up, and function in a healthy way. God's plan for His people cannot be fulfilled unless we gather locally so that the apostles, prophets, evangelists, pastors, and teachers can equip us to effectively work in His kingdom.

Relationship #6: Community
Result: Momentum

"To the angel of the church in Ephesus, Smyrna, Pergamum, Thyatira, Sardis, Philadelphia and Laodicea write" (Rev. 2: 1,8,12,18; 3:1,7,14).

God calls us to form coalitions of life-giving churches in order to fulfill the Great Commission of Christ to His disciples. By doing so we can:

1. Pray for every single person in our community at least once a year.
2. Communicate the Gospel in an understandable way to every person in our community at least once a year.
3. Add at least one percent of our city's population to those attending church on an average weekend, by the end of each year.

For our city of Los Angeles, one percent of 4,000,000 people means an additional 40,000 people should be saved and discipled within our churches citywide every year. If each of the 2,283 churches here within the city would disciple 17-18 people, by God's grace that 40,000 number could easily be reached. And for a small house fellowship like ours, with 50-60 people, that would be at least one soul saved and discipled every two years. That's a slam-dunk if we have a true spirit of community among us. But if we think we're the only real church, then we'll go year after year after year without adding a single soul to that number. To achieve these goals, churches must coordinate citywide efforts together. Individually, no church could ever accomplish this alone.

Just as individual Christians must connect with others in a healthy local church in order to grow strong, so local churches must connect with other local churches in order to become increasingly more effective.

Relationship #7: <u>The Universal Church</u>
Result: Completion

"After this I beheld, and, lo, a great multitude, which no man could number, of all nations, and kindreds, and people, and tongues, stood before the throne, and before the Lamb, clothed with white robes, and palms in their hands" (Rev. 7:9).

Finally, the set of relationships needed to empower us for effective ministry is the network of relationships we as local churches form to enable missionary activities. These efforts require local churches to take a portion of their tithes and strategically use the money to ensure that every person living in our generation has an opportunity to hear the Gospel. To fulfill this task, we must work in harmony with the other members of the universal Body of Christ in increasingly broader and broader relationships.

By working as members of the universal church, the community church, the local church, small friendship groups, and our own family settings, we can see Jesus' calling on our lives fulfilled. Some will argue against various levels of these increasingly empowering relationships. However, I believe as we receive the revelation of God's Spirit and the Scriptures about our purpose in His kingdom, it becomes evident that each of these relationships are vital to His purpose and dependent upon one another. Relationships are not optional for any of us as Christians! Productive, empowering relationships make ministry delightful and efficient with maximum breadth of impact and are so foundational to building a life-giving church.

Reflections in Marriage

1. The Divine Proposal (Bride)

THE REAL THING:

The Church as the Bride of Christ finds her fulfillment in Christ. Its members are the very body of Christ. Aside from the mere social clubs some churches have devolved into, the authentic church is totally preoccupied with her identity in Christ.

"...we are members of his body, of his flesh, and of his bones" (Eph. 5:30). It stands to reason that the members of the body of Christ should only be for Him. Here in materialistic America it's harder to tell that the church actually finds fulfillment in Christ, because so much "success" is measured by brick and mortar, by people and popularity, or in dollars and cents. But even here, it's those believers who are obsessed with their Savior who truly live lives "separated unto God" (Rom. 1:1; 12:2). If there's any other motive driving separation than an obsession with the Lord, then what's called church is not the real thing. "Know ye not that your bodies are the members of Christ? Shall I then take the members of Christ and make them the members of an harlot? God forbid!" (1 Cor. 6:15).

THE REFLECTION:

The woman finds fulfillment in her husband. Obviously Christian wives find their first fulfillment in Christ, just like Christian husbands do, but there's a distinctive fulfillment women find in complementing their husbands that parallels the distinctive satisfaction the church finds in serving Christ. Again, don't forget the type or picture of who wives represent in marriage—the Church.

"If you can find a truly good wife, she is worth more than precious gems! Her husband can trust her, and she will richly satisfy his needs. She will not hinder him, but help him all the days of her life. She watches carefully all that goes on throughout her household, and is never lazy. Her children stand up and bless her; so does her husband. He praises her with these words: 'There are many fine women in the world, but you are the best of them all.' These good deeds of hers shall bring her honor and recognition from even the leaders of the nations" (Living Bible; Prov. 3:10-12,27-29,31).

How-Tos" For Couples

Our CHILDREN: Her Happiness!

A huge part of Rachel's happiness was her children. They were not playthings to her that she used for her own satisfaction but real, live souls in whom she found tremendous delight. Remember, Rachel did not marry until she was twenty-eight years old and our oldest was not born until after she was thirty. She lived a number of years as an adult before experiencing the joy of motherhood. Yet she did not need children to complete something in herself; she truly loved her children for *them*, not for herself.

R __elationship _____ More than she loves you, she loves this.

C __onnection _____ Talk about yourself or don't bother getting married!

O __penness _____ Remember, she is body modest, but soul naked.

C _hildren _____ Give her as many of these as her heart desires.

C _____ Tender words, gentle touch, and a good ...

F _____ Share these: What's hers is yours.

F _____ This comes along with the marriage.

Plus M _____ The wonder of it all.

It didn't occur to me when I was outlining these seven items that the "children" aspect of her happiness would be listed right in the middle: three before and three after. But that's really the way it was. Rachel's children were central to her happiness.

Notice I didn't say, "Give her as many as her body can produce" but rather "as many as her heart desires." Rachel was very satisfied with her five. Certainly her heart was saddened by the anti-children mentality prevalent in our culture, but she held to a circumspect view and was content with how the Lord led us in it. And boy, what an awesome grandmother she would have been too! Somehow still, I think she probably gets to know each one of our grandchildren as they come along even before I do. She's with the Lord, you know, and children come from Him.

Because her children brought so much joy to her heart, and because she believed the Scriptures, Rachel took child training seriously. Proverbs 30:17 says, "The eye that mocketh at his father, and despiseth to obey his mother, the ravens of the valley shall pick it out, and the young eagles shall eat it." She did not want eagles eating out the eyes of her children! Many times folks have asked us over the years, "How did you transfer your values to your kids?" For her, it really came down to her relationship with them. Since she was a homeschool mom, she obviously taught them many things extraneously, too, but her most profound influence came through the relationships she nurtured with each one of them. This was her genius, and she loved it.

Asher and his mother.

Since Rachel's children meant the world to her and were the source of so much of her happiness, it tickled her immensely when I moved toward them too—played with them, read to them, and held lengthy conversations with them. Of course, I did so because I, too, have a huge heart for my kids, but making my wife happy in the process brought exponential value all around. So, I would say to every husband out there, "Go for it!" Your wife will honor you!

In summary, there are four basic options for mothers in our society today. I'll list them in their order of preference. 1) Those who want to stay at home with their kids instead of getting a job outside the home, and can. 2) Those who want to stay at home with their kids instead of getting a job outside the home, but can't. 3) Those who don't want to stay at home with their kids and would rather get a job outside the home, and do. 4) Those who don't want to stay at home with their kids and would rather get a job outside the home, but can't. The best possible scenario is the first one, and that's where Rachel was as a mother. She absolutely loved her role as a homemaker, so that's where she chose to work and invest most of her time. And she was one of the happiest mothers the world has ever known!

CHAPTER 6

Pretty Grown Up

Rachel's Story

From the moment of her birth, Rachel possessed a stunning beauty that only seemed to intensify as she developed and matured. I know, I know—I'm biased! But anyone who knew her, or simply saw her, has to admit there was something naturally beautiful about her. Ok, you don't have to admit it. But it's true! And like I said in the first chapter, I know because her daughters were "spittin' images" of her at that age, as Aunt Pearl used to say.

Interestingly, part of her beauty was the sense of reservation she carried about herself. Somewhat shy and sheepish, she was never quite sure what people thought of her, and so she was never quite sure what she thought of herself or even what she thought of them, for that matter. This made her somewhat mystical. In part, it was this mysteriousness that made her attractive, I thought. With that slightly slanted grin suspiciously on her face, the mystery was complete. It was always there! In every circumstance, in any situation, whether she was hustling about the house, quietly resting, or being transported into the little helicopter that carried her away, in which moments later her heart beat its last, there was the same mystique, the same shyness, the same pretty.

Junior High class picture

So it comes with a bit of surprise to many that this is the modest, reserved young lady who boarded a single-prop Cessna at nineteen years of age and flew off into the brambly bush of northern Ontario to teach first and second graders at the Poplar Hill Development School. It was a place only accessible by plane, and for six to eight weeks at a time during both the fall freeze-over and the spring break-up, not even the planes could get in or out. They had to use either pontoons or skis. When the lake was neither water nor ice, but something in between, all of the residents of Poplar Hill were essentially stranded. (This, of course, was long before the days of cell phone towers, or even land lines up there in the bush.) No email. No Facebook messaging. No skype. No texting. It was just you and the Lord and those around you, communicating with the outside world through prayer.

She'd grown up, pretty much, by then. And those three years in the North would prove to be significantly formative for her. Her supervisor and mentor, Emma Huber, would speak profoundly into her soul during that term of voluntary service (or solitary service, as the case may be) there in the Northwoods. A passionate lover of her family, Rachel constantly carried her Mom and Dad and her brothers and sisters close to her heart. During those long winter days with very few daylight hours, the loneliness she felt was sometimes unbearable. She longed for a soulmate with whom she could share her heart and thoughts. It was into this fertile field of friendship that Ms. Huber was able to sow deep seeds of quiet contentment. She reminded Rachel that there would never be a Prince Charming who would be able to meet the deepest longings of her heart. Keeping Jesus first-place in her heart was the only real antidote to a life of lonely isolation.

Her Inspiration

But eventually Rachel's soulmate would come. Here's what I composed for her two months before asking her to marry me:

RACHEL (Valentine's Day 1984)

If I'm singing a song or humming a tune; If I'm reading or even if writing ...
The song's much more sweet and the writing more fine—If I'm doing it, Rachel, with you.
If I'm going to church, or coming back home; If I'm hiking or if in a Cutlass ...
The trip's so much nicer, the mere ride is a charm—If I'm doing it, Rachel, with you.
If I'm washing the dishes or playing a game; And the same if I'm making a pizza ...
The time goes a flying and it's so satisfying—If I'm doing it, Rachel, with you.
Be it skiing or shopping or visiting friends; Whether out in the cold or inside ...
Let me say it again that the time that I spend—Is SO pleasurable, Rachel, with you.
When we're studying, praying, or just having a chat; When we're laughing, or maybe we're crying ...
Just to be with you, Dear, is so much of a cheer—Yes, I love it my Sweetheart, with YOU!

The Bride of Christ

So when is the church mature? What does it mean for the Bride of Christ to be pretty grown up? Is it ok for the Bride of Christ to be pretty? What does an attractive church look like? What about mature? Can the church be both mature and attractive? Can it really be one or the other?

Let's consider maturity for a bit.

Acts 9:31 says, "So the church throughout all Judea, Galilee, and Samaria had peace, being built up and walking in the fear of the Lord and in the encouragement of the Holy Spirit, and it increased in numbers." I see six signs of maturity here.

1. **Far-reaching.** The church is described here as having already reached *"throughout Judea, Galilee, and Samaria."* This is both a comment on geographic and cultural boundaries. People were carrying the gospel to various regions and various types of people. To say that the church existed in Judea was expected, but to see it spreading among the Samaritans was not. Many of the early believers were ethnically Jewish, and they did not associate with the Samaritans. This signals to us that we must seek to increase the parameters of the church in this world despite cultural, ethnic, economic, and social differences. We should never hesitate to push beyond man-made boundaries when sharing the gospel of Christ.

   Mature churches are not obsessed with themselves. Instead they get over themselves and beyond themselves with long-range views. Rather than gorging to obesity, they are outreaching and visionary, keeping fit with rigorous evangelistic exercise. In the first chapter of Philippians, Paul talks about how his persecution and imprisonment led to the "furtherance" of the gospel. Most Greek dictionaries define the word "furtherance" *(προκοπή -- prokopē)* merely as progress or advancement. But Warren Wiersbe in his "Be" series says it's more than mere progress. Instead it is a pushing forward, penetrating kind of progress—the kind that frontier pioneers do, or like the advance troops of a military incursion.

2. **Peace.** The church *"had peace."* I think this is a commentary both on how they existed in the culture and how they treated one another. Think, for a moment, about what it means inside a

church family for there to be peace. It is when there is unity amidst diversity. Control-hungry participants are seen for who they are, whether leaders or lay-people. Instead of pandering after mere performance and artificial uniformity, we pin our unity on the idea of working toward reaching the whole world with Christ, honoring Him as Lord, and living in His daily presence as the friend He says we are. When this is our mission, then genuine unity is recognized, true peace is realized, and spiritual maturity is the result.

3. **Development.** This verse also tells us that the church was *"being built up."* King James used the word "edified." The Greek words used in the phrase find their regular usage in the construction of a house. The church was growing up. The right pieces were being put in the right place. It was a sign that strength was being added to the structure, so a healthy fellowship could follow. The outward ministry was coupled with inner growth. For a church to mature, it needs both internal and external development.

As missionaries of the gospel we should see ourselves as something like scaffolding on a building project. Our goal is to develop a structure that can stand alone. Once it can do that, the scaffolding is taken down and moved to the next building development. And every one of us is a missionary. We should not see ourselves as digging in for the long haul. We're on the move. Really, we're pilgrims. Not hermits holed up for good, nor nomads wandering around unsure of where we're going. We're pilgrim missionaries. We know where we're going, and we know what we're looking for. Ultimately we're "seeking a city that hath foundations, whose builder and maker is God" (Hebrews 11:10).

4. **Holiness.** As the church developed, it was *"walking in the fear of the Lord."* I love this phrase because it signals the depths of what living holy is like. Though holiness includes morality, it is not the sum total of holiness. Rather, holy living is a lifestyle in which the awe of God is carried with you at all times. The church, as it was in those days, should be marked by the holy presence of God. Our behavior is changed by our view of how different God is from us. Consequently, our transformation by the gospel means that we are now set apart for the Lord's purposes and that we experience everyday joy in the process.

Holiness and living in the fear of the Lord should not be a dull, joyless life. Perhaps that's why Paul asked, "Where is that joyful and grateful spirit you felt then?" (Galatians 4:15). One of the holiest and most mature things we can do is choose to be happy. I think of our neighbor lady back in International Falls, Minnesota, who often said about any given day, "If it's not a good day, I make it a good day!" Certainly this should be the choice of the people of God. It's easy to become overly task-oriented as a church and give in to a get-'er-done, check-it-off-the-list mindset. Everything and everyone can soon become projects. Any sense of levity soon disappears. We need to create a portal of praise, again as the Apostle Paul instructs us in Philippians 4:4, "Always be full of joy in the Lord."

5. **Encouragement.** Knowing that we are called to holiness, encouragement becomes natural because the church receives *"the encouragement of the Holy Spirit."* He indwells believers so that, individually and collectively, we can be bold in both ministry and mission. On your worst day when the whole world seems to be caving in, the Holy Spirit has the desire to encourage you. When church life is at its toughest because of temptations from without and trouble from within, the Holy Spirit never abandons us. The God of the universe wants to encourage the church.

Mature believers in the body of Christ don't depend upon external circumstances or outward signs and wonders for their encouragement. Instead they draw upon the Holy Spirit's encouragement from within. King David did this one time when he was returning with a band of his brothers back down to his retreat in Ziklag, in the south country of Judah (1 Samuel 30). Ziklag was to David the equivalent of Camp David to our presidents here in America. But when David got there, he discovered that the Amalekites had invaded the town, burned it to the ground, and made off with their wives and children.

Properly so, the entire group owned their grief and together, it says, they all "lifted up their voices and wept, until they had no more power to weep" (vs. 4). To make matters worse, the people threatened to turn against King David (apparently blaming him for their problems) and spoke of stoning him. Of course, David "was greatly distressed," but it says "he encouraged himself in the Lord his God" (v. 6). From the strength of such intrinsic encouragement, David rallied his fellows to stage a counter-attack and totally routed their enemies from Ziklag, completely recovering not only all of their stuff, but more importantly, every single one of their wives and children as well (vs. 18-20).

Quite early in my ministry, one of my overseers decided I needed an assistant and brought in a man totally unprepared for the hard stuff of church leadership. He was so self-conscious and intimidated by others that he spent most of his time in a slump, stewing about why he was even there. I had to spend much of my time keeping him propped up emotionally. My assistant could not assist, because it took more assistance to assist him than what he had in himself to assist me. All because he lacked the emotional maturity to "*encourage himself in the Lord his God.*"

6. **Growth.** Everything we've observed in this text, so far, leads us to what we see described in here now in how the church "*increased in numbers.*" Through mutual ministry within the church, and by their ministry to outsiders, the church grew. We must be unashamed in our desire for the church to grow numerically. It is totally biblical that God wants more people converted, more people experiencing grace, more people ministering, and hence, even more people coming to know Him as Savior. The church should want the same and should work with everything we have to see it happen. A mark of a maturing church is that it focuses on the kind of ministry that will persuade people to accept the truth of the gospel and the beauty of knowing Christ.

But again, growth is both internal and external, in that order. An increase in quality is an increase in quantity. Milton, a young brother in our church in Minnesota, used to pray a beautiful prayer so often in our church there. It was an essential prayer. He'd pray, "Lord, help us not to grow only in numbers, but in grace and maturity too." At first it made me nervous, because it seemed he was downplaying numbers, and my Bible says God is not willing that any should perish. But the more he prayed that, the more I realized how crucial that prayer was, because if we're not growing up on the inside, we'll hardly do well on the outside either. We may manage to make some kind of an external show, but unless it represents a quality of character, both personally and as a body, it will only be "wood, hay, and stubble" (1 Cor. 3:12; 2 Tim. 2:20).

Reflections in Marriage

2. The Importance of Leaving (Bridegroom)

The second thing we notice as a reflection of Christ in marriage and His relationship with the church is how important it is to *leave*.

THE REAL THING:

Christ left heaven in order to establish His church. "And the word was made flesh and dwelt among us" (Jn. 1:14a).

He was at home in heaven, at one in the trinity, with all of eternity at His feet. Yet He left it all for love ... to embrace the bride He'd give His life for. "[Christ] made himself of no reputation, and took upon him the form of a servant ... and being found in fashion as a man, he humbled himself" (Phil. 2:7-8).

THE REFLECTION:

Men, too, must leave the security and comforts of home and their parents in order to marry their bride. "For this cause shall a man leave his father and mother" (Eph. 5:31a).

All former loves and interests must be left behind in order to maintain true fidelity—time-consuming business interests, hobbies, and anything else that would separate men unnecessarily from their brides. Christ gave up everything for us. So, as bridegrooms, we must lay everything else aside in order to give ourselves fully to our brides.

The church then, too, has a respons(ibility) to leave as well. It's a response to Jesus' willingness to leave heaven for her.

"How-Tos" For Couples

Our CONVERSATION: Her Happiness!

"Hold tight to the sounds of the music of living ..."

This line epitomized Rachel's happiness in so many ways! I cannot recall it without barrels of tears. She specifically requested "We Have This Moment" be sung at our wedding reception in Dakota, Illinois, thirty years ago this fall. We've sung it dozens of times as a family in the years since. To Rachel, simply LIVING was music, and while she loved to worship each Christmas around the lofty cadences of Handel's Messiah, it was the simple songs of everyday living that moved her most:

> *The laughter of her children at play,*
> *Holding hands while we ran through the sweet fragrant meadows,*
> *The tiny voice of her little girls calling,*
> *Her little sons running there on the hillside,*
> *The blue of the sky, the green of the forest,*
> *The gold and the brown of the freshly mown hay,*
> *Add the pale shades of spring and the circus of autumn,*
> *And she viewed a lovely today!*

R _elationship_____ More than she loves you, she loves this.
C _onnection_____ Talk about yourself or don't bother getting married!
O _penness_____ Remember, she is body modest, but soul naked.
C _hildren_____ Give her as many of these as her heart desires.
C _onversation__ **Tender words, gentle touch, and a good ...**
F _____ Share these: What's hers is yours.
Plus M _____ This comes along with the marriage.

Strategically centered, the middle line of the song said it all for Rachel: "Tender words, gentle touch, and a good ..." Bill and Gloria Gaither had written "cup of coffee," and Rachel certainly appreciated the aroma of those words, but to her, it all spelled CONVERSATION. A good conversation! This was her kind of world. Small group discussions were a close runner-up. She never cared to talk in front of crowds, though she did do it some, and she didn't especially like being in crowds period. But heartfelt, one-on-one conversation was the crown to her happiness!

For most couples, the guys need to talk more and learn the art of conversation. But for me, I needed to learn how to "zip it." Because, although Rachel was not a woman of many words, the words she spoke were voluminous! And it takes two, you know, to make a conversation. I'd tend to get excited about something she'd say and start running away with many words, but the next thing I knew it was a monologue instead of a dialogue. So I learned to sprinkle my words out very carefully—well-placed, inquiring, interested words that would draw her along instead of drown her out. Ah! What rapturous conversations we'd have then! They were the building blocks of our intimacy.

So, for most of you husbands, it may be the other way around. You may need to up the ante of your words a bit. But be encouraged, it doesn't have to be many words. Just a few sincere words scattered here and there. Your wife NEEDS them! Please give them to her. Your investment of words in conversation with your sweetheart will yield dividends beyond your wildest dreams.

CHAPTER 7

The Bride of Christ

Rachel's Story

Long before Rachel was ever my bride, she had become the bride of Christ and was loyally awaiting her eternal wedding day. Never would we have thought it would be so soon, but that was who she was, the bride of Christ, fully engaged, wedding garments on, awaiting the marriage supper, looking forward to full consummation. She had accepted His invitation of love to join Him in His life and mission for the cosmos. 1 Peter 3:1-6 described her well:

> "In the same way, you wives must accept the authority of your husbands. Then, even if some refuse to obey the Good News, your godly lives will speak to them without any words. They will be won over by observing your pure and reverent lives. Don't be concerned about the outward beauty of fancy hairstyles, expensive jewelry, or beautiful clothes. You should clothe yourselves instead with the beauty that comes from within, the unfading beauty of a gentle and quiet spirit, which is so precious to God. This is how the holy women of old made themselves beautiful. They put their trust in God and accepted the authority of their husbands. For instance, Sarah obeyed her husband, Abraham, and called him her master. You are her daughters when you do what is right without fear of what your husbands might do."

She put her trust in God, in Christ her spiritual Bridegroom. She belonged to Him, there was no question. She didn't need me to give her meaning and purpose in life. She already belonged to SOMEONE, and she was at rest. If I would have been an unbeliever, I could not have been so for very long, because her godly disposition spoke voluminously to me. Her pure and reverent life would have won me over. She didn't need a fancy hairstyle, expensive jewelry, or beautiful clothes to draw me in. Obviously to me her natural beauty was helpful, but even if I would have been blind and deaf I would have been drawn to her spirit, an inner quality that came from the deep well of her soul, the unfading beauty of a quiet and gentle spirit so precious to God.

Now ladies, please don't feel inferior to Rachel. She was not perfect. She was not always quiet and gentle. There were times she tried to use the effect of her words and the force of her will over mine, and it did help to get my attention sometimes. One time she hit the dining room table so hard with her fist that it knocked over the salt shaker, just to make her point. But her most powerful persuasion came from something deep within—a passionate, loyal reverence for God that she allowed to splash over me as well. A true daughter of Sarah she certainly was. Perfect she was not. So don't feel inferior. Real godliness in a bride isn't so much about perfection as it is about passion—a passionate heart for her Bridegroom.

The King James translation of I Peter 3:3 says, "Whose **adorning** let it not be that outward **adorning**." According to Strong's Greek Lexicon, the word adorning is *kosmos*, which means "a complete, orderly, harmonious system." We men are more planetary in our approach to life. In fact, we're so singular and disconnected we appear wandering and erratic at times. But for a woman, it's cosmos—everything tied together and related to each other. Every single piece of her world affects everything else. For many of us men, if the colors of our clothes don't match, it's no big deal, but for most women, they must match. Not only their clothes, but their hair, the complexion of their skin, and the style of their pocketbook, purse, or handbag. Their cosmos even includes their home: wall colors, furniture, flower arrangements, and whether the bedroom closet doors are fully closed or not. All a man cares about is his own planet, if that. But women are cosmos conscious. It *all* matters to them.

Our 25th wedding anniversary (photo taken by our children with secret plans to have a black and white pencil sketch made of it).

When the Holy Spirit was inspiring Scripture, He cautioned women about their cosmos. He inspired Peter to write that the inner cosmos matters more than the outward, that true adornment is an inside-out sequence, and that if the spirit is beautiful, the body will be, too, without artificial, man-made makeup. "Man looks at the outward appearance, but the Lord sees the heart" (1 Samuel 16:7). This was Rachel's focus, and she taught her daughters the same. She was engaged to Christ in such a way that brought her entire cosmos together with such composure that she appeared beautiful even when she was tired, sick, or first getting up in the morning. This is also why, when I first saw her body in death, it was not the tubes hanging out of her nose and mouth nor her physical wounds that turned me off—it was that her spirit was gone. She was now my bride no more, but the bride of Christ forever!

Her Inspiration

Discovered recently in my email history was this heartwarming reminder of Rachel's admiration and support for me expressed in response to an email from John Ivan Byler, back in early August 2012, three months before I lost her. John Ivan is the secretary of the Biblical Mennonite

Alliance for which I had been asked to preach a message at the annual summer convention. One of the things the convention leaders do for their speakers is offer critiques of their messages in an effort to help them improve. I'd opted for this because I like to be open to constructive criticism. Rachel had found some of the critiques a bit trivial, particularly the one about me putting my reading glasses on and off too often while I spoke. So when I received this encouraging note from Brother John Ivan, I forwarded it on to her for her own encouragement as much as for mine. You can follow the email thread below, starting with her response back to me:

---------- Original Message ----------
From: Rachel Witmer rhwitmer@hotmail.com
To: Ernest Witmer ernestwitmer@juno.com
Subject: RE: Thank you for the message!
Date: Tue, 7 Aug 2012 11:57:40 -0500

What an encouraging note! You're the BEST! :-)

--Forwarded Message Attachment—
From: jibyler@hotmail.com
To: Ernestwitmer@juno.com
Subject: Thank you for the message!
Date: Mon, 6 Aug 2012 19:24:44 -0400

Biblical Mennonite Alliance
August 4, 2012
Dear Brother Ernest,

One week ago the BMA was gathered in Harrisonburg, VA, for our annual convention, a time of refreshment, fellowship, renewal of friendships, spiritual input and challenge for all who attend. You filled an important role in that gathering as you preached on the theme "How Does Transformation Happen?" on Saturday evening. We appreciate your willingness to prepare and share in order to bless and challenge our people in a spiritual way. On behalf of Brother Todd, the Board of Executors, and the entire Alliance, I express to you our sincere gratitude for your ministry to the Lord and to us. I noticed many positive evaluations of your message in the evaluation forms submitted. Thanks be to God for His word and His messenger!

May God bless you and your work in His Church!

"Therefore, my beloved brethren, be steadfast, immovable, always abounding in the work of the Lord, knowing that <u>your labor is not in vain in the Lord</u>." 1 Cor. 15:58 NKJV

Sincerely in Christ,

John Ivan Byler

BMA Administrative Secretary

I treasured Rachel's response way more than I did even John Ivan's and held it close to my heart for weeks. Three months later she was gone, never again to provide such living encouragement to me. Yet her words linger on in the museum of my memory as an unspeakable inspiration!

The Bride of Christ

My experience with Rachel as my bride has taught me so much about what the Bride of Christ, the church, should be. I'll list ten things to start with, beginning at the bottom with number ten and working back to number one:

10. She was <u>beautiful</u>. This is the end result of who Rachel was, not the beginning. Without the inner qualities that truly made her beautiful, she could have looked like she was made in Hollywood but still be as ugly as a weathered fence post. So it is with the church; you can have everything "right" on the outside but be totally lifeless within, which ends up equaling ugly. But it takes life to recognize life. A dead corpse can lay next to another dead corpse forever and never recognize it for what it is. That's why there are no conflicts in cemeteries. But if you're truly alive, you know the difference. A living body will energize you, but a corpse will turn you off.

9. She was <u>wise</u>. Rachel had the gift of discernment. She was able to see through stuff like nobody else I know. She could see through me, she could see through her kids, she could see through other women, she could see through teenagers, and she could see through

most of what goes on in the name of the church. The reason she could do this was because she was willing to self-evaluate, to see through herself by being transparent with others. Again, the true church is the same way. It is possessed with Holy Spirit insight. The true church is in touch with reality. It's not living in a dream world of what it wishes was real, but it accepts the world as it is and brings everyone and everything to Jesus because He is the total summation of what is real and true. Ephesians 4:21 says, " ... the truth is in Jesus." The true church has a humble, transparent ability to be real about itself, to self-evaluate, to determine if it is truly representing what it says it is.

8. She was <u>merciful</u>. Nothing accounts more for the marvelous impact Rachel had on my life for over twenty-eight years. Certainly, she could see right through me, but she did so with a heart of mercy. She knew my faults were not what I wanted in my life, and so she did not allow them to define me for her. Rather, she saw me in light of who she knew I *wanted* to be and who I *could* be in Christ. Psalm 85:10 says, "Mercy and truth are met together; righteousness and peace have kissed each other." This is an imperative couplet. Mercy without truth is less than real mercy; peace without righteousness will not result in real peace. In the same way, truth without mercy is not real truth. Because the truth is, everyone can become exactly what they should be in Christ. And real righteousness produces peace. If it doesn't, it's not really righteous. This is how the church should be too.

7. Rachel was <u>practical</u>. Even though she was an idealist, she knew that if she could never be happy unless things were perfect, she'd never be happy. As her husband for many years, I'm sure grateful she was practical about me. She knew that she could not be married to a man who was called to serve God and expect him to only serve herself, and so she gave me the freedom to put God first, knowing that the practical outcome was going to benefit her too, because God has quite a bit to say about how a man should serve his wife. The same is true with the church. As churches we must be able to call folks into a full and vibrant relationship with Jesus Christ, knowing that there is really no other way for them to benefit the church. But if we put their relationship with the church ahead of their relationship with Christ, we not only hurt them, but as a church we're shooting ourselves in the feet.

6. Rachel was an <u>idealist</u>. Even though she was practical, she knew that she needed an ideal to aim for. Without a goal, she knew she could never make progress. And so she entertained lofty goals that led her along through life. I used to tease her about her many lists, but she would counter that I could be more organized if I kept a list too. My response was that I had a mental list. But you know how that goes—the busier you get the more difficult it is to remember everything on your list. Churches, too, need to have ideals to work toward. Of course, our greatest ideal is Jesus. Because we're not exactly like Him today, nor will we be completely like Him tomorrow, it helps tremendously if we keep Him in focus as our perfect ideal. The same way with the Scriptures: we want to obey all of the Word of God. It is our standard. Unless we appreciate it as something worth obeying, we'll never experience its eternal value.

5. Rachel was <u>orderly</u>. Not only was she tidy about her own person, but she was also a neat housekeeper. But she didn't obsess about these things; she just kept them in balance. She had a routine, and she was good at keeping it. She loved to go to bed in good time and get up early. One of the first things she would do in the morning was read her Bible. Even if it didn't immediately put her on a spiritual "high," she'd faithfully spend time with the Lord just because she loved Him. Most churches think it's important to have a systematic theology, but they forget about a sympathetic relationship with Jesus Christ—not in the sense of feeling sorry for each other, although that certainly does characterize how Jesus feels toward us in all of our struggles, but more in the sense of being in a congenial relationship with Him. He longs to have a vital relationship with us, and so as churches, this should matter even more to us than having all of our theological ducks in a row.

4. Rachel was <u>cautious</u>. There was nothing impulsive about her. I was the risk-taker in our relationship. She weighed things carefully and arrived at balanced conclusions. That's why it seems so strange that she would be killed in an auto accident by pulling out in front of a pickup truck. The very fact that she lived an appropriately cautious life causes everyone who knew her to know beyond the shadow of a doubt that here had to be some extenuating circumstances. The church of Jesus Christ should never be seen as careless. We should be careful and considerate in how we relate

to others, and we should also be careful in how we handle the Word of God. We shouldn't make it say more than it does, nor less. And we should "live circumspectly, not as fools ... but as wise, redeeming the time" (Eph. 5:15-16). Also we should make very deliberate decisions about building redemptive relationships with unbelievers.

3. Rachel was a <u>servant</u>. Her first love language was "Quality Time," but her second was "Deeds of Service." The second best way for me to love her was to find some way to serve her interests. In the same way, one of the best ways she could think of if she wanted to express love to me, or to someone else, was to provide some practical service to us. She was the doer of many good deeds. Not out of some sense of performance, but from the genuineness of her heart. It should go without saying that one of the best things a church can do is to serve others. Too often churches focus on what people should believe or not believe. Rather, churches should focus on what people need and then go about meeting those practical felt needs in the context of the Gospel. Some of their needs are material. Other needs are emotional, or filial, or social. Of course, they also have spiritual needs, but many times they do not feel those spiritual needs until the lower levels of their felt-needs are met.

2. Rachel was a <u>friend</u>. Her primary love language was "Quality Time," and so she loved spending time with people she cared for. She loved to spend time with me. She loved to spend time with her children. She loved to spend time with her friends. And the time she'd spend with them would be quality time. She wasn't into just carelessly throwing time away. She was careful to spend meaningful times together with them. So with the church; there's no point in just going through the motions of doing church. Let's do truly meaningful things together. Let's worship sincerely and enthusiastically. Let's serve each other with carefulness and kindness. Let's consider one another deeply to know what makes each other tick and how to "scratch where it itches." And then let's extend the same to others in our community who may not be a part of our fellowship.

1. Rachel was a <u>lover</u>. Before everything else, Rachel was the love of my life. We loved each other, and it's amazing how mutual love grows. When I first decided to pursue her in courtship, I expressed in very

elementary terms my love (interest) in her. When she responded favorably, that made me love her even more. When she responded to even more love, my love for her just kept getting deeper and deeper until I decided I wanted to marry her. That's the way love works. In the church, we also need to remember just how powerful genuine love is. It's the beginning of all other virtues. The more we love each other, the more we love each other. We love Jesus because He first loved us. The same in the church. We love each other because we feel loved by each other. So, whatever else happens, let's make sure that others feel our love!

Reflections in Marriage

2. The Importance of Leaving (Bride)

THE REAL THING:

The church must leave the world.

"Be not conformed to this world, but be ye transformed" (Rom 12:2a).

"Love not the world, neither the things that are in the world" (1 Jn. 2:15a).

It's not a begrudging thing. It's just as strange to think the church of salvaged souls would have any hankering for where they came from!

In representation of this, there is a leaving necessary on the bride's part too. What bridegroom wants a bride who drags her feet to the altar? If you're a bridegroom, can you imagine marrying someone who really wishes they could just stay at home where they were?

THE REFLECTION:

If a woman marries, she must leave parents and family. This involves learning to trust her husband's decisions, rather than defaulting to those of her family. It involves learning to treasure his counsel and opinions and learning to lean on him emotionally. As with the bridegroom, so with the bride—all former loves and dreams must be left in order to be a faithful lover and companion.

"...for whither thou goest, I will go; and where thou lodgest, I will lodge: thy people shall be my people, and thy God my God: Where thou diest, will I die, and there will I be buried" (Ruth 1:16-17).

"How-Tos" For Couples

Her FRIENDS—Our Friends: Her Happiness!

"Rachel, Rachel, Rachel!" The chant still surprises me when I remember it from ten years ago. We were walking into Rachel's thirtieth high school reunion in Freeport, Illinois. Apparently someone saw us coming and decided to do what I'm sure they had to know would embarrass Rachel with the unexpected publicity.

"Shall we run and hide?" I suggested in jest.

"No, it'll be ok," she replied with the characteristically crooked, goofy-mood grin she'd use when she knew she was being played with. "I guess this is what old friends are for!"

R _elationship____ Husbands: More than she loves you, she loves this.

C _onnection____ Talk about yourself or don't bother getting married!

O _penness_____ She is body modest, but soul naked.

C _hildren_____ Give her as many of these as her heart desires.

C _onversation___ Tender words, gentle touch, and a good …

F _riends_____ Share these. What's hers is yours.

F _____ This comes along with the marriage.

Plus M _____ The wonder of it all.

Back in 1974, Rachel would probably never have won an award for most popular person in her class, but you'd have never guessed it now. For some reason it seemed she was the classmate to be celebrated in 2004. It wasn't because she had so MANY friends, just REAL ones. If you'd have spent twelve years in the same classroom with her, you'd be her friend too. That's the way she was. You'd be her friend even if she was not yours. She lived the proverb from one of the oldest biblical manuscripts, the Textus Receptus: "A [wo]man that hath friends, must show [her]self friendly" (Prov. 18:24, KJV). She had friends because she was friendly, and because she had friends she was friendly toward them.

Rachel's friends meant the world to her! If you were her friend, you didn't need me to tell you that—you already knew. She wasn't dramatic or gushy about it, just solidly there. You'd have had to seriously violate her trust to change that. She was loyal. But if you were not her friend, then you might have needed me to tell you, because she would never have told you that.

There were a half-dozen times or so in the thirty years I knew her when she risked losing a friend in order to be a REAL friend. She trusted the proverb also that says, "An open rebuke is better than hidden love! Wounds from a sincere friend are better than many kisses from an enemy" (Prov. 27:5-6, NLT). She'd summon her courage, pray like crazy, and dare to confront someone she cared deeply about ... but even then, you couldn't miss the friendliness that begged for expression in her demeanor. She just couldn't help but be friendly. So she had friends—deep, long-term, committed friendships they were.

And since Rachel was mine, her friends were mine. And this made her happy! I knew that anyone who was Rachel's friend was a friend worth having, even if we didn't necessarily click naturally otherwise. Today, even after she's gone, I have many friends whom I'd never have had without her. So to all of you friends out there—thank you for being a friend to Rachel, and thank you for being my friend too.

CHAPTER 8

Teacher of the Years

I need to be careful here lest my family and I lose our sympathy support from those of you who feel sorry for us living in the city. We actually have the best of both worlds here, because Los Angeles and its surrounding suburbs is not a typical metropolis. For example, Los Angeles proper has only half the population of New York City but twice the land area. So we have only twenty-five percent of their population density, at least in some parts of the city; other parts are more on par. When you consider all eighty-eight suburbs together with the city itself, we are spread over 5,000 square miles.

One day I loaded up a book display to install in a CVS drugstore down in Rancho Santa Margarita, a city south of us in Orange County. It was about a sixty-mile drive, but I never left the city. I made my way through creepy-crawly traffic, but I also sailed along at freeway speeds up and around mountain ridges and down through bush canyons. It's all mixed together in what we call the city of the Angeles.

Just off the south end of the Saddleback Mountains in southern Orange County is a high point, known as Santiago Peak. Running up toward that peak is a canyon called Holy-Jim Creek Canyon. At the bottom of the canyon is the creek, at least when it's rained enough to create a creek, and at the top end of the creek is the waterfall. Running alongside the creek and sometimes switching back and forth is a trail named Holy-Jim Creek Canyon Falls Trail. How would you like a name that long? On that trail then was me, hiking and hiking until I reached the falls, twelve miles round trip.

I had dedicated the rest of the day, after setting up the book display, to hiking up to the foot of the falls so I could sit there, meditate, pray, and write. I wrote the major part of the first section of this chapter, *Teacher of the Years,* which tells some of Rachel's story as a teacher. The second section is an inspirational piece for both women and men to "follow [her] as she followed Christ." It's a testimonial of how God's presence became so real to her through rainbows. And then a later section of this chapter again provides some challenge for the church to BE the beautiful bride of Christ that Rachel modeled so well as a bride herself.

Rachel's Story

Rachel never won the national Teacher of the Year award from the President of the United States of America, but there are a number of U.S. citizens, students of hers, who I know would give it to her in a heartbeat. She certainly qualified for Teacher of the Years because of the number of years she taught in a number of different and challenging environments. She taught in both Canada and the United States and in both government and private school settings. Last, but certainly not least, she was mother and homeschool teacher to all five of our children, falling just two years short of seeing her youngest son Christopher through his high school graduation before she was killed. Not surprising, being the teacher and mother she was, her oldest daughter Carita took up the profession and picked right up where Rachel had left off and guided Christopher through to the end.

Miss Rachel Schrader
Teacher's Aide

Rachel as a first grade teacher at the Poplar Hill
Indian School in northern Ontario.

Rachel found so much personal satisfaction in teaching that it really gave her pause when I proposed marriage to her in the spring of 1984. In spite of writing in a letter to her parents in February 1984 that I had told her, "I believe our relationship has a future" and in spite of acknowledging to them, "I like him lots," she was still deliberating the implications of needing to say "no" to the school board about coming back to teach the next year. That's how much she liked teaching—just about as much as she liked me! Her parents encouraged her to not teach the following year if she thought our relationship was getting that serious. In another letter to them, she reported that "Ernest liked your advice." It goes without saying that my feelings for her were fast becoming more *love* than *like,* but the proposal still had three months to wait.

Rachel excelled at teaching the ABCs of ACE first-grade class. Every set of parents within the communities in which she taught wanted Miss Schrader to teach their kids how to read. This was, in large part, why we chose to homeschool when our children came along. Rachel was so concerned about them having a solid reading base from which to build the rest of their education that she didn't want to outsource it to anyone. She would do it herself! And so began the Homestead Learning Center we came to call our little homeschool. All of our children read well today and are insatiable readers. Hence also, each of them has become an adventure author to one extent or another. If you appreciate good reading, you usually end up writing well too.

Asher's high school graduation from our Homestead Learning Center. The graduation was held at our home in Upland, California.

Her Inspiration

When God Wants to Hug Me, He Sends a Rainbow
By Rachel H. Witmer

God said to Noah, "I have placed my rainbow in the clouds. It is the sign of my permanent promise to you and to all the earth." I have a rainbow story too ...

Sometimes I have struggles. Sometimes I have fears—big fears. I have fears about the future, fears about money, fears about my family. My family—what if something happened to them? What if one of them would get really sick? That seemed too overwhelming. I recoiled at the very thought. What if God took Ernest? I would be all alone. Oh, how tight I held onto the fears. But God began to whisper, "Trust me."

One morning the struggles were especially intense. I was crying out to God; I was pleading with God. After a while I felt my heart surrender. Later that day I jumped in the van and ran up town. The Christian radio station was tuned into Moody Bible Institute. Pastor Joseph Stowell was speaking. He quoted the verse, "I will never leave you nor forsake you." He repeated it several times. Those words went deep into my heart. The evening of that same day, we as a family were returning from a ball game. As we drove through town, a rainbow appeared. It was a BEAUTIFUL rainbow! It was complete from one end to the other and such colors! Not only was there one—it was double. There were two complete rainbows more beautiful than any I had ever seen! While we exclaimed about the rainbows, my heart remembered the verse God had given me earlier that day. It seemed He was saying to me, "I still keep my promises."

In the succeeding days and months, God would give me that verse over and over. It popped up in the things I was reading, in sermons, in prayers. It came in many ways at times when I least expected it, and He sent more rainbows.

The message began to take root. I began to believe it with all my heart. I felt God's love.

The verse and the rainbow were OUR special thing.

Then one day it happened. I received a call from the doctor—Kristi's MRI showed that she does have a tumor in her brain. Oh, Father, I can't do this. I CAN'T!

One day when we were in Illinois, we were driving with Grandpa and Grandma (my parents) to go see some friends. I sat in the back of the van. Someone spotted the ends of a rainbow. We watched and the whole rainbow emerged.

Grandma exclaimed, "We don't usually see such brilliant colors," and I knew that God had just whispered to me, "Yes, you can handle this, because I am with you."

Two weeks later we traveled home after spending the day with doctors, listening to their diagnosis, discussing some of the options. My heart was heavy with the weight of it all. Music was playing; it was dark outside. Suddenly I became aware of the words they were singing—"I trace the RAINBOW through the rain / And feel the PROMISE is not vain / That *mom* (morn) shall TEARLESS be." **God can even send rainbows in the dark!** What an awesome God!

Two days later at a ladies retreat, we sang that same song. I pondered again this message from God. Another day we received an e-mail from a friend who shared about a time one of their children had medical problems. She wrote, "Whenever we had a bad day, which was often, we would look for a rainbow, because when Noah was in the ark God gave him a rainbow." A rainbow! I think when my Father wants to draw **this** child close and give her a hug, He sends a rainbow. I love rainbows and I LOVE HIM!

Rainbow picture taken by Rachel's sister-in-law Lynette Schrader near Rosedale, Ohio, soon after Rachel's death. Rachel loved rainbows!

Yes, God Puts Rainbows in the Sky

Let me share this testimony from our daughter-in-law. Thanks, Teresa, for sharing this with us.

> Yesterday afternoon Asher and I were driving through the rain and saw an incredibly vivid, complete rainbow. We noticed that it was starting from the hills of the Forest Lawn Cemetery where Mom Witmer is buried. We had a moment of awe.
>
> Later that evening I was telling Carita and Kristi about the rainbow, and they excitedly wondered if we had read Phil Beiler's status on Facebook (he lives with their family). We hadn't. But yes, I got goosebumps when I heard where the other end of the rainbow was.
>
> Phil wrote, "Never in my life have I seen the end of a rainbow, but this afternoon I saw a rainbow literally coming out of our house. It was brilliant and complete. From one side of the sky to the other, starting at our house. Amazing!!!"
>
> "Thank you, Jesus," Teresa goes on, "for this beautiful rainbow today and Your faithful promises. And I can't help but say, 'Thank you, Rachel Witmer,' because I kind of wonder if you didn't have something to do with it."

So there you have it. God put another rainbow in the sky in memory of Rachel, to be seen by two parties, one at one end of the rainbow and the other at the other end. And so fitting to who she was as a person—her home was always where her heart was and even from beyond the grave she is remembered with one end of the rainbow in Forest Lawn Memorial Park where her body rests, and the other end resting right on the house where her family dwells and where the warmth of her heart is still felt.

Evening Bible Camps were done in honor of Rachel in 2013.

The Bride of Christ

Boaz and Ruth

The most romantic story of God's provision for companionship in the Bible is the story of Boaz and Ruth. There are so many things about this ancient account that provide riveting inspiration yet today. Four highlights in particular catch my attention:

1. I love how this courtship was so clearly rooted in godly character. Unlike most dating couples whose relationship is merely the product of human nature and natural attraction, for this couple it was all about recognizing God's divine influence in each other's lives. Even the fact of the huge age difference speaks to the supernatural element of this romance. Jewish tradition holds that Ruth was forty years old and Boaz was eighty. Forty years difference! It's in almost the same genre as marrying someone from a different ethnicity, which this was as well, or marrying someone who's handicapped. It's right up there with the beautiful love story of Nick Vujicic and his wife Kanae Miyahara.[1] These kinds of relationships take

---

[1] "Love Without Limits: A Remarkable Story of True Love Conquering All." Nick Vujicic and Kanae Miyahara.

something much greater than human compatibility. They are inarguably nothing short of divine arrangements! Godly character was a given; compatibility, an adventurous journey of love.

2. Another thing I admire about this godly affair is the obvious motivation that was involved. For both Boaz and Ruth, it was all about giving—not getting. All Christian couples like to give lip service to this ideal, but if God were to lay bare the actual intentions of the heart, I wonder how true it would be? Please don't misunderstand me here: I believe it is GOD who puts the longing for companionship and intimacy within every heart. The challenge is simply to be real about it. Let's not put ourselves forward as pursuing some sort of lofty ideal when in reality we're simply responding to God's natural investment in our hearts from Creation.

    Having said that, it's quite clear from the biblical text that Boaz and Ruth were extraordinary in their selfless intention ... and it's absolutely beautiful! So much so that at one point Boaz actually hands off his own interest in Ruth to his fellow kinsman who might actually have had more right to her than himself. Can you imagine that? How many of us would be willing to give our cousin first choice to the one we love? Nevertheless, I can't help but hear his sigh of relief when his kinsman declines. But note again the stark contrast of the cousin protecting his own collateral interest over the personal benefit he could have provided to Ruth. In my book, Boaz has to be one of the greatest lovers of all time! Give, give, give ... provide, provide, provide ... protect, protect, protect; his true motives were made clear by his actions!

3. Their goals were noble. It's refreshing again to notice especially that Boaz was looking toward the value of a long-term commitment for Ruth's benefit. He knew that's what would be best for her. In contrast, the spirit of our day reeks with so much selfish lust as guys try to get their girlfriends to live with them without the security of marriage. It's all for their own personal benefit and gratification without taking lifelong responsibility for the one they seek pleasure with. Such transparent neurosis should be obvious, but alas, many woman, especially immigrant women, are taken advantage of in this way.

But even Ruth as the newcomer was poignantly pure in laying out her goals to both Naomi and Boaz. In a very short time, the biblical text indicates, it was clear to "all the city" that she was "a virtuous woman." She had shown more kindness in the long run than she had even at the beginning when the natural person would think she was trying to give a good first impression. But she had proven to all that her heart was pure in that she did not chase after young men, "whether rich or poor" (Ruth 3:10-12). The average woman would have been affected both by his age and by his social standing. But it was clear to Boaz that neither played a part in her demeanor.

4. Finally, notice the results! When the original idea is God-fearing instead of humanistic, when the motives are about giving and not getting, and when the goals have an eye toward long-term commitment rather than short-term pleasure, the results will produce a profound blessing. All the way around, there was peace with all the pieces. There was praise to the Lord. And there was overwhelming goodwill among the relatives. Even the embittered Naomi was given by her lady friends a whole list of reasons for her to bless the Lord as "a restorer of life, a nourisher in old age," and they saw her daughter-in-law bearing a son as more of a blessing than if she had born seven sons herself! There was total joy all around, pure and simple! A win-win-win for everyone!!

Now contrast this all to what would have happened in today's normal environment. King David with his selfish pursuit of Bathsheba also provides a pathetic counterpoint.

1) At the intersection of shallow passivity and naked beauty lies an abundance of natural temptation. Wandering around after dark, David stumbled across more than most men could manage. Any ideas originating from this juncture were bound to lead to catastrophe. His shortsightedness is breathtaking!

2) The self-centered plotting to get Bathsheba for himself is a direct contrast to the selflessness Boaz demonstrated in giving to Ruth. The way in which David manipulated the circumstances and used his power and position to satisfy himself is the epitome of immaturity. And this guy was called a king?!

3) What were the goals? How could they be more graphic? He reeked with self-absorption! His own personal pleasure was his single goal. He totally objectified her; obsessing over her body with no thought for her person. He could not have revealed more disdain for himself in the process. What a horrible self-image!

4) The results were devastating, heaping hurt upon hurt toward everyone around. "The sword shall never depart from thy house ... I will raise up evil against you from out of your own house ... your wives will lie with your neighbors in broad daylight ... the son born from your sin will surely die" (2 Sam. 12:10-14). No hint of blessings; just hideous loss for everyone.

Reflections in Marriage

3. The Importance of Cleaving (Bridegroom)

THE REAL THING:

Christ showed cleaving commitment for the church in various ways.
"I will build my church" (Mt. 16:18).
"I will not leave you comfortless" (Jn. 14:18a).
"...the church of God, which he hath purchased his own blood" (Acts 20:28).

THE REFLECTION:

Husband must cleave committedly to his wife.
"For this cause shall a man ... be joined unto his wife" (Eph. 5:31b).
A divine order: One cannot cleave until he leaves. Leaving is for the purpose of cleaving. The Hebrew word suggests the idea of being glued together. Not like tape but an inseparable bond taken apart only with great difficulty and damage. The same is true of persons "glued" together in marriage. Cleaving obviously excludes marital unfaithfulness.

"How-Tos" For Couples

Her FAMILY: Her Happiness!

Finally, in answer to the question posed to me a while back by two fine husbands: How do I connect with the heart of my wife? I said, "Just make her happy!" But what does just making her happy look like? What did it look like for Rachel? Seven points:

R _elationship_____ Husbands: More than she loves you, she loves this.
C _onnection_____ Talk about yourself or don't bother getting married!
O _penness_____ She is body modest, but soul naked.
C _hildren_____ Give her as many of these as her heart desires.
C _onversation____ Tender words, gentle touch, and a good ...
F _riends_____ Share these: What's hers is yours.
F _amily_____ This comes along with the marriage.
Plus M _____ The wonder of it all.

Certainly not least, though I've listed it last, before the bonus point. I could never write about what it took to make Rachel happy without making a big deal about her family. Of course, our own family made her very happy, too, but I'm talking now about her family of origin—the Schrader family.

Obviously no family is perfect, but family systems are fascinating to observe and better yet to experience. We're all involved in at least three family systems. Each of us inherently participate in both of our parents' family systems, plus the one they've created for us. And if we're married, we've embraced still another three: each of our spouse's parents' family systems and the one those parents made for him or her. (This is why in-laws matter!)

Add to these six systems a seventh, which we develop with our marriage partner, making the circle of family systems complete. (Plus then there's the potential for the challenging dynamics of blended family systems because of remarriage, which we all hope we never have to encounter, yet some of us no doubt will.) But it's this seventh family system that becomes the primary one for our children, and the one for which we as their parents are directly responsible.

It's the second set of three systems I embraced when marrying Rachel. It came with her. I didn't just get *her*, but I got her family systems too.

And what mattered most is that I really needed to "get it!" I needed to understand her family and fully appreciate who they were and what made them tick. I needed to learn why they think the way they do, what their history was as a family, and how they got to be who they are. Rachel was a product of these systems, and if I was asking her to marry me and my systems, I also needed to marry hers. She was willing to embrace my family system and I needed to embrace hers too. In fact, I would suggest it was more incumbent upon me to embrace her family system before expecting her to embrace mine.

As a whole, it was a fun experience for me. The Schraders were so different than the Witmers in some interesting ways. I remember the first time I saw them all tuckered out after a through-the-night drive from their farm in northern Illinois to Blackduck, Minnesota, where Rachel was teaching and where I was frequently coming to date her. Her family was lying all over the living room floor of "the shack" where her sister Miriam and Clovis lived at the time. I'd never seen such a thing before! I was used to my family sitting up nice and straight in the living room; the only time we laid down somewhere was in our bedrooms—on the beds. But I caught onto this rather quickly and as our children could all testify, I probably spent more time with them on the living room floor playing games, watching a movie, taking naps, or just chatting than sitting with them on the sofas.

Of course some systemic issues coming both ways from our families of origin were more challenging. And as typical human beings, it would have been easier if the other would change, not?! But if we can self-evaluate at all, our observations about our own family systems and those of others should teach us something about ourselves. Like a hanging mobile, we tend to make room for ourselves and accommodate our own ways quite fluidly. But we find it much more difficult to accommodate and make room for others. You see, we all see ourselves as normal but everyone else as abnormal. And the more different they are from us the more abnormal they seem. But over the years, Rachel and I found that if we were truly honest about our own systemic weaknesses and were committed to growth and health within the family system we were creating for our kids, it was a win-win for everyone.

I've often wondered since Rachel's death why the Lord saw fit to take her home at the critical point in time that He did. Perhaps it was because He wanted her life on this earth to end at its zenith of happiness. She was so excited about her whole family arriving in Canon City for the wedding. Not only were all of our children converging there for Asher and Teresa's wedding that weekend, but her parents were coming and most of her siblings too. SHE WAS A VERY HAPPY LADY! So she went from a zenith of happiness here on earth to the ultimate epitome of happiness in heaven, to be not only with other family members who'd gone before, but all together FOREVER with JESUS! The rest of us? Well, we're not quite there yet, but we're on the way!!!

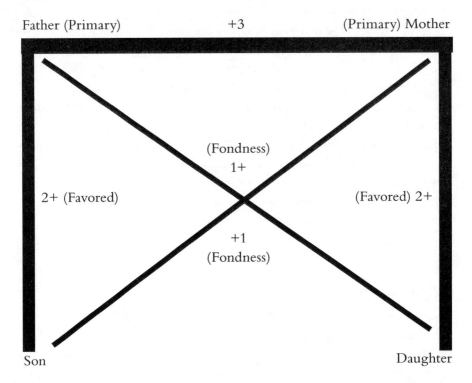

Father (Primary)　　　　　　+3　　　　　(Primary) Mother

(Fondness)
1+

2+ (Favored)　　　　　　　　　　　　　(Favored) 2+

+1
(Fondness)

Son　　　　　　　　　　　　　　　　　Daughter

The strongest relationship in the family system should be the husband/ wife, father/mother relationship. We can call this a 3+ relationship. It should not only be the strongest, but also the most intimate. Everything else in the family hinges upon the strength and intimacy of this relationship.

The second strongest relationship should be the father/son, mother/ daughter relationship. This is a 2+ relationship. It's a favored relationship, not in the sense of there being "favorites," but in the sense that it's the same gender and so there is a natural favorability between mothers and daughters and fathers and sons. Little boys naturally want to grow up to be like their dads, and likewise little girls want to grow up to be like their moms. Girls tend to play "mom," and boys tend to be "dad" in their playing.

The third strongest relationship is the father/daughter, mother/son relationship. It's a 1+ relationship. But it's a relationship of fondness. The fondness is born out of (again) the children watching their parents. Girls notice how fond mom is of dad and grow up thinking, "I'd like to have someone like dad some day." And boys notice the fondness their dad shows toward their mother and so they too think, "Wow, I'd like to have a special lady in my life some day, too, that I can feel such fondness for."

When these values get mixed up, confusion is the result. If there is a lack of true intimacy and strength in the husband/wife, father/mother relationship, one or the other will tend to draw someone else in too close. If a father draws a daughter in too close or a mother draws a son in too close to fill the void they feel from the lack of intimacy in the marriage relationship, same-sex confusion can be one of the outcomes. So then rather than daughters feeling favored by their moms and a fondness for their dads, or rather than sons feeling favored by their dads and a fondness for their moms, they feel this strange favoring by the opposite sex where instead there should be a naturally fond attraction toward.

CHAPTER 9

My Bride

Rachel's Story

It all started when I was invited to attend a wedding as a traveling companion to the boyfriend of the bride's sister. I didn't know this ahead of time, but Rachel and her family would be singing at the ceremony the next day. I first saw her during rehearsal the night before. She—the most striking of them all—was standing there behind the podium with her beautiful sisters, her parents, and her brothers. And what do you know, your humble servant was called upon to provide some feedback from the auditorium regarding the sound and balance of the four-part harmony they were performing. I was delighted for the interaction!

The journey continued at Maranatha Bible School sometime later. One afternoon I was sitting in the library studying, writing, and minding my business when I looked up and out of the full-length glass window into the hallway. At that very moment, Rachel walked past the window on her way down the hallway. I had seen her around the school before, but this is the moment that remains transfixed in my mind as to when my desire for her began.

Later that evening, in "The Little White House" dormitory where twelve of us fellows lived in the little berg of Lansing, Minnesota, during that cold winter term, I asked one of my dormies, "Do you know Rachel Schrader?"

"Yes," he answered.

"How old is she?" I pressed.

"Oh … I don't know. Maybe 23 or 24," he provided.

My third question startled him a bit: "Why isn't she married?"

"Well … I don't know," he stammered. "Ah … yea … that's a good question. Maybe it's because guys are scared of her."

I could certainly understand why guys might be nervous around her—in fact, I was trembling a bit just thinking about it, but I knew right then-n-there that I would do whatever it would take to overcome any fears standing in the way of at least getting to know Rachel some more. I was still very young, barely eighteen myself, so I knew I wouldn't be pursuing a relationship with her just right away, but maybe, just maybe, God saw her as part of my future. I could live a long time simply dreaming about that one!

And so it came to pass, as love stories go, that in the process of time I'd occasion to meet her yet again. This time it would be at the wedding of the friend I'd questioned so abruptly in The Little White House in Lansing.

★★★★

The wedding was over and the reception was winding down as well. I stepped through the kitchen area of the reception hall as a shortcut to the restroom. On my way back through, I spotted her, quietly waiting for something or someone beside the kitchen door. Was that someone me? I could only hope so!

"Why, hi, Rachel," I exclaimed. "It's been awhile. How are you doing?"

"I'm fine. How are you?"

"Very good," I replied. "Especially since seeing you here!"

I could see her blush ever so slightly. "What would you think of spending some time together yet this evening?" I ventured. "Could I take you out this evening?" I was trembling inside.

"Uh … thank you," she said, "but I'm currently in a correspondence relationship with a fellow from Maryland I met a couple of years ago in VS," she said hesitantly.

"Oh! I'm sorry," I said. "I didn't know that."

"I don't know what the future holds …" she acknowledged bashfully.

We hesitated a bit, smiled at each other, and then went our separate ways. But the thing that resonated so clearly in my heart and mind that afternoon was the honorable and respectful way in which Rachel had interacted with me that day. Nothing she said or did gave me any reason to feel embarrassed or regretful, or that I was somehow out of place in expressing my heart for her as I did. She seemed confident in who she was, and because of that, she had no need to diminish me. I went back to my home in Wisconsin and pondered these things in my heart.

But life's road always wends and winds, sometimes with hairpin turns, valleys to wander, and uphill stretches to climb. I dated another girl for a year, only for us to end up breaking up with each other. To this day, I'm convinced I would rather have a girl disappoint me than me to disappoint her. It was not dramatic, but difficult nonetheless!

I then enrolled again at Maranatha, this time for a full year and a full load of classes. Besides my conversion and my eventual marriage, nothing has set the direction of my life as much as that decision. I was determined to seek God with my full heart, soul, mind, and strength! Three classes were required per term as a minimum to attend, but I never took less than four, and for two terms, I took five. I'd get up at 5:00 every morning to study and often got special permission from the dean to study after lights-out at night. I was a frequent occupant of the furnace room (where the dean relegated me so as not to disturb anyone), sometimes till midnight.

It was in that context of intense seeking and study that John Coblentz asked me to consider coming to northern Minnesota to teach in their small Christian school. I would live with them and house-sit for them when they were gone for weeks at a time in itinerate teaching ministry from state to state throughout the country. I consented, thereby setting the stage for Rachel to re-enter my life, or more accurately, for me to re-enter hers.

I have to confess (shh! don't tell John) that part of my thought process in accepting this teaching assignment in northern Minnesota was that I knew Rachel would be up there, too, teaching at Blackduck in the Kitchi Pines School just two hours away from International Falls. I had heard by the grapevine that she was finally free from all other suitors "and engagements whatsoever" and was enjoying her teaching career to the fullest. Two questions now remained: 1) How do I focus on teaching while at the same time pondering what God might have in mind for me in marriage? and 2) How do I convince her to yet consider one more guy, especially when she was so totally "engaged" to her teaching?

North I went, away from my home community in Wisconsin where I was born and raised, up into the Icebox of the Nation to teach in a small Christian school not far from Rachel. My parents had sold the dairy farm and moved to Phoenix a couple years earlier. Soon after arriving in northern Minnesota, I attended a joint Labor Day meeting of all the northern Minnesota Mennonite churches. After dinner, there in another dining hall not many miles from the one where I had first talked to her about a date some three years earlier, I met Rachel again. Not totally by accident, but not really planned either. We chatted briefly, and then I excused myself to go join the others who were gearing up for the traditional softball game afterwards. (Rachel later told me how comfortable she found herself to be in talking to me and that I didn't make her feel awkward in knowing how to engage with me in that brief encounter. She subconsciously marked it down for me in the "plus" column of her mind to be referenced later, even though at that point she didn't have a clue about all this Ernest guy had in mind.)

That was in September.

★★★★

Each Thanksgiving season, the northern Minnesota Mennonite churches banded together to put on a youth rally at the Kitchi church. This was the event I was angling for as a good time to begin courting Rachel. Remember, she had turned me down once because she was busy corresponding with another guy from Maryland. Now she was fully engaged in her teaching career with first and second graders and totally enjoying it … and I later learned from her that she was pretty much done with guys! I had my work cut out for me!

Why, you might be asking, was I so attracted to Rachel anyways? Well, to begin with, she was beautiful! Stunning, I thought. But I honestly didn't know that much about her besides her quiet, steady disposition and the grace with which she walked. What I did know said a lot to me about her. We'd been around each other some at Maranatha Bible School and although we had just one class together, as I recall, I always wanted to be very careful and clear when speaking up during discussion times in that class. Years later Rachel told me she always appreciated what I had to say in that class and the way I seemed to know what I believed and why. Another thing that attracted me to Rachel was that she was an inside-to-outside kind of person. What you saw on the outside was even more who she was on the inside. She was beautiful outside; she was even more beautiful inside. She was somewhat quiet on the outside; she was even more calm and serene in her spirit. She carried herself with poise and grace on the outside; she was even more so at heart.

Besides that, Rachel was my perfect complement. I am someone who has a hard time thinking without talking (or writing). She was someone who could not talk unless she had fully thought things through. (It's not hard to tell from that which one of us got into the most trouble!) I am outgoing; she was more reserved. I am a risk-taker; she was always careful.

I love crowds; she avoided them. I can get lonely, even in a crowd; she could feel crowded, even when alone. (I'm sure she could have handled this widowhood thing much better than I. But I'm glad she didn't have to!) Yes, there were times during our marriage when we wished we were more alike. As Dr. Marlin Howe used to say about most couples, "What attracted me to you now turns me off," so it was with us at times. But we also knew we were good for each other, and we complemented each other so well. I'm convinced that's part of what made us a good set of parents. We knew our kids needed us both. In fact, while we were so opposite in many ways, besides our common faith and worldview, our thoughts and convictions about children and child training was probably our greatest unity. It was very attractive to me to know that from her years of teaching, she'd make a tremendous mother. And did she ever! It was such an honor to be married to Rachel. She broadened my life, enlarged my heart, and deepened my thinking tremendously over twenty-eight years of marriage, to such an extent that living life without her now feels like I'm barely half here.

But now I'm getting ahead of my story.

Another part of what attracted me to Rachel was that she was on a journey. She had not arrived! She hadn't fully grasped where all God was taking her, but she knew what she was looking for. And what she was looking for had everything to do with finding her ultimate security in Him. She was leading a compelling life, and I felt led to accompany her.

So I wrote the letter.

No, it was not a letter to HER ... not yet. That would follow. This one was to her pastor, Brother Val Yoder. Just a kind of reference letter inquiring about her. Val assured me of her integrity and faithfulness as a member of the Kitchi church and assured me of his full support. He also gave me her father's phone number when I asked for it. You see, even though the Schrader family lived in Freeport, Illinois, they had moved their church membership to the Kitchi Pines church in Minnesota, because it was more in keeping with the direction they wanted to go as a family.

Calling her father Ron was my next move.

Now I had never attended a Gothard seminar yet, but I knew from my own values and upbringing that I certainly wanted the involvement of her parents in our relationship. I'll be the first to admit I've not always followed God's principles as closely as I should have. But this much I knew, even then, that all of God's principles are quite well ruined if legalistically applied. So it wasn't so much the "precise maneuver" I was interested in by contacting her father; rather, it was that I wanted to know his heart, and I wanted him to know mine. In some circles today, there is this idea that if the guy first contacts the father of the girl he's interested in, all potential problems dissolve. It completely misses the point! The objective has to be deeper than that. It's not the exact procedure that matters. Instead, it's the intent and integrity of the heart: the guy's heart, the parent's heart, and most significantly, HER heart. And, by the way, if a father is afraid of some guy running off with his daughter's heart, it's a sure sign HE certainly doesn't have it! But if he truly has his daughter's heart, he won't need to be uptight about it, and it will be obvious both to him and to her, and to everyone else, long before she's old enough to date.

Recently one young married man told me his story of how he had talked to three different fathers over a period of several years about dating their daughters. In each case, they had given him their permission, but when it came to asking the daughters, each one had turned him down. So he said to me, "I decided, I'm done with this whole thing of talking to the father first!" And when, during a term of voluntary service at Northern Youth Programs, he later met the girl he would then marry, he simply got right to the point, talked to her about his interest in starting a relationship with her, and then later called her father for his counsel and advice. Whatever the sequence, it is REAL honor and communication that matters, not the putting forward of some impression thereof.

At twenty-seven years old, I knew Rachel knew she didn't necessarily need her father's "permission" to date. She was a mature adult and had proven her honor to her parents long before. Nevertheless I wanted to hear his father-heart for her. Eleven months later, I'd also sit down and talk with her parents about my plan to propose. And over the next twenty-eight years, there were many, many times I'd talk to them about her, about me, about our marriage, about our family, and about their hearts for us as her parents and as grandparents to our children. Even now, after Rachel's safe and secure in heaven with Jesus, I still frequently talk to her parents about her.

So it was on a Wednesday morning when I called her father Ron, introduced myself to him, and shared with him my interest in his daughter Rachel. He didn't know me, but he'd heard about my family. And in typical Mennonite-game fashion we soon had an entire array of mutual acquaintances we could connect around. I was well on my way toward making the most important phone call of my life.

Two days later, on Friday morning, before heading out of the house to conclude another week of teaching my twelve students at Northwood Christian School, I picked up the phone and called Rachel. She was just ready to head out the door to wrap up her week of teaching first-graders at Kitchi Christian School near Pennington.

"Hello Bylers," came the voice at the other end of the line. It was Clovis Byler answering the phone. (Rachel lived with Clovis and Miriam, her sister, in what they all called "The Shack," a modest little cabin along The Scenic Highway.)

"Yes, hello Clovis. This is Ernest Witmer calling from up here at Northwood. You remember we met briefly at the Deeper Life campground on Labor Day?"

"Yes! Yes, I remember," he responded. I could already envision the trademark smile spreading across his face. "So how are you doing, Ernest?"

"I'm doing great!" I tried to sound brave and confident while the cordless phone shook in my hand. "I was wondering if there'd be any chance I could talk to Rachel?"

By now his smile had penetrated the very timbre of his voice. "Oh, I'm pretty sure there'd be a chance you could do that," Clovis replied. "She was just about ready to leave for school, but I think she'd take time for a phone call from you. Here she is!"

"Hello?" Her voice sounded soft and curious. (I'd told my mother years before that I didn't agree with the old saying, "The way to a man's heart is through his stomach." My opinion was, and still is, that the way to a man's heart is through her voice. Just short of a lisp, I LOVED the way Rachel pronounced her words, and her sweet melodic cadence made it even better.)

"Hi Rachel," I offered. "I'm looking forward to coming down for the youth rally in a couple of weeks, and I'd be honored if you would join me for a dinner date that Saturday evening." I waited awhile before continuing. "I can call you back next week, because I'm sure it'd be good for you to take some time to think and pray about it."

"Oh!" she said. "This sounds interesting. I'll have to give it some thought. Yea … why don't you call me back again next Friday morning about this same time?"

"Ok! Great," I said. "I'll do that. In the meantime … have a wonderful week!"

Ah! That didn't go too bad, I thought to myself. *And I really like the sound of her voice on the phone. Actually she sounded kind of excited,* I continued to muse, almost out loud. *But wow, a week seems like an eternity!*

What I didn't know at the time was that, right after my call to her Dad on Wednesday, he had promptly called her yet that day. So she had been pondering and praying about this for a couple of days already! And she had pretty much made up her mind to accept my date. But she wanted to pray some more about it, and (modest as she was) she didn't want to come across as too eager.

But it was all good! I really didn't mind waiting, because "waiting time is not wasted time when you're waiting on the Lord." Or when you're waiting on your wife, or your girlfriend, or on the one you'd like to be your girlfriend and possibly your wife someday. Waiting is good!

So I waited … and prayed. And prayed … and waited. And then I fasted … for three whole days and three long nights. But that made the time go even slower. Each day seemed like a month. I was so excited! But too much excitement without absolute knowledge is kinda silly, isn't it? But that's called hope, and according to the book of Romans, "hope maketh not ashamed." And Hope is Rachel's middle name. (But I didn't know that yet either.)

The next Friday morning dawned bright and clear. Novembers in Minnesota can be bone-chilling, to say the least, as Rachel and I and our little newborn Carita would learn a couple of years later after moving there from Illinois where we spent the first two years of our marriage. I still remember the minus 40 degrees we experienced there that first year, living in a thin-skinned trailer house with two primary survival tasks to be completed each day: 1) chopping firewood and 2) crawling underneath the trailer house to thaw out the frozen water pipes. We finally discovered if we simply vented the clothes dryer into the crawlspace and let it run for an hour or so, that would thaw the pipes too. But this November morning was different. There were still lots of fall colors surrounding the house, the sun was shining brightly in the east-side dining room window, and the temperature outside was a perfectly comfortable 70 degrees with your parka on.

"Let's see," I thought to myself. "She was just ready to leave for school last week when I called, so I better call a few minutes earlier this time. I don't want her to feel pressured for time."

"Hello, this is Rachel speaking." She answered the phone on the first ring.

"Why, hello, this is Ernest calling back. Glad to hear it's you that answered the phone ... thought maybe Clovis or Miriam would answer again."

"Yea ... they're usually the ones that answer the phone, and they teased me about answering and telling you I wasn't available. But they were nice and just told me to answer it. How was your week?"

"I've had a good week. Seemed like a long one, and hard in some ways. I spent some time fasting and all. But it's been good! So what are you thinking by now? Wanna go out for dinner together the Saturday evening of Youth Rally?"

I could feel my heart thumping through my shirt and then it nearly jumped right out when I heard these words: "Yes! I think that would be special."

And thus it began ... a courtship that would be fulfilled in marriage eleven months later with an extra special journey through Itasca State Park at five months for the confirming proposal. There was much we discovered about each other during those bi-weekly dates in the intervening months, not the least of which was that we had so much in common. The things that really matter in marriage were so obviously there: commitment to the Lord, devotional lives that reflected an open relationship with Him, a history of active Christian service, a love for and regular interaction with children, honorable relationships with our parents, and interpersonal dynamics with a host of friends, any of whom would give ready and frequent testimony as to who we really were.

Oh! Did I mention how stunningly beautiful she was? I know you're gonna declare that's a non-essential, but I really believe it's an important aspect. Remember where beauty resides? First of all, true beauty is in the spirit and physical beauty is in the eye of the beholder. And it needs to stay that way! As the Rev. Howard Hendricks says, "You choose your love, and then you love your choice." Every groom can rightfully declare his bride to be the most beautiful. But in my opinion, mine was especially so. I remember my mother telling me, "You probably better not marry someone you can't stand to look at across the breakfast table every morning." I knew I could do that very easily. In fact, I was pretty sure I could sit there gazing all day long at Rachel's face, not only across the breakfast table, but the lunch table and dinner tables, too, and all the day through!

★★★★

Sitting there in a quiet corner of Itasca State Park on a little bench at a bend in the trail, I turned and looked into those beautiful dark brown eyes and coined a term that would stick with us as an everyday expression of endearment. "Honeybunch, will you marry me?" I said.

Rachel always said I surprised her with the question that day, and I really believe I did. Not that it was completely unexpected, just not expected on that day, because we had planned a picnic for THAT day! You see, Rachel could be a romantic (we have five children to prove it), but she was also a very practical soul. She loved to be scheduled and organized. We had been planning this picnic for several weeks, but I had gone to great lengths to make it seem somewhat tentative and casual. I had several parks in mind for the picnic that day and wanted her to end up being able to pick the one she'd like the best for this occasion, but I didn't want to reveal my plan. So as we were driving out the Scenic Highway still deliberating about which park it would be, I turned the car around twice, heading toward a couple different parks. I wanted to appear anything but deliberate as we tossed the options back and forth in our discussion. I was concerned that if we drove straight to Itasca State Park—the obviously most romantic option—it would appear too organized and planned and would give away my intentions to pop the question that day, which I was sure would be how she would anticipate it.

This was in May of 1984, and we would get married six months later in October. Back in February she had written to her parents, "Ernest says he believes our relationship has a future. But it's only been three months since we began dating. Can a relationship that develops so fast really last? I hope so, because I like him lots!" So the proposal wasn't a complete surprise to her, we now know from the letters her mother recently gave me. Surprised, or not surprised, I will never forget the slightly crooked grin that played across her lips that early afternoon, nor the gently lilting tone in her voice when she responded with, "Yes, Ernest! Let's get married!"

Right then and there we sealed the deal with a formal little document expressing our love for each other and our commitment to follow through with marriage. In the previous year, seven different couples we knew had become engaged and had subsequently broken their engagements. While we knew that was not the kind of relationship we had, we wanted to make a point of reversing those kinds of outcomes in our circles.

I took her hand in mine as we strolled out to the car to get our picnic supplies. Such a delicate hand! So soft and small and slender it felt to me. It was the hand of my Honeybunch! Her hand was mine, and mine was hers. And I would hold it thousands of times more in sickness and in health, for rich or for poor till death did us part on the Life Flight stretcher where I held it last as it was … still soft and small and slender. But now no longer mine as she became all His forever!

Now as we carried our picnic basket back to build a small campfire for roasting the burgers we'd brought along, we began to plan for our wedding. Would it be yet that fall? Or winter? Or would it be a springtime wedding, a year later? We didn't know for sure yet. All we knew was that we loved each other deeply and that we were getting married!

That summer seems very distant in my memory now and a bit hazy. I know we both finished out our terms of teaching at our respective schools. Then we traveled down to Freeport, Illinois, together, caravanning with Rachel's sister Miriam and her late husband Clovis Byler. We had barely headed down the road until we hit a deer with my car along the way and quickly came back to Clovis' mom's place to skin it out and put it in the deep freezer. My twin brother got married in Missouri in early June, as did Rachel's sister Ruthanna later that same month. Plus we travelled together (with Grandpa Graybill along as our chaperone) to Harrisonburg, Virginia, to attend the wedding of Rachel's best friend Anna Slabaugh as well. It was a very busy summer for all of us, but especially for Rachel's parents with two weddings three months apart, somewhat premonitory of the two weddings in our own family 28 years later, when our two sons got married only six weeks apart.

I also remember staying up late at night together—Rachel and I—designing our engagement announcement and wedding invitations. Both were hand-designed and photo copied in black print on sky-blue paper, including the engagement photo. These were sent out in homemade envelopes, typical of the practical, efficient, domestic-oriented lady Rachel always was. Just like the Proverbs 31 woman we read of in the Bible.

Speaking of the Proverbs 31 woman, for humor's sake I have to insert a story here about Rachel and the down-to-earth way in which she could identify with so many other women out there who struggle with the impossible ideal this lady from ancient Scripture seems to hold out.

Just months before Rachel's passing, she was driving our minivan with Carmen, one of the younger women from our team, in the passenger seat. They were talking about all the demands of being wives to visionary men, housekeeping, mothering, and ministry when Rachel pounded the steering wheel with her fist and declared, "I hate Proverbs 31!" Carmen hoots with laughter every time she retells this story, and so do I because I can just see Rachel doing that. Not because she actually hated the Bible or any of the books of the Bible or any of the women in it, but because she truly knew how to identify in an everyday way at a practical level with other earthlings. She also had a list of five things she hated about being a pastor's wife—good biblical points—but that's for another chapter.

Amidst all the hustle and bustle of wedding plans and everything else included, our wedding day finally arrived. October 20, 1984. For the next twenty-eight years and beyond, that date was etched in my mind and heart like no other date. Just seeing the letters and numbers written either in print or in longhand still makes my heart skip a beat. Such a landmark, such a fork-in-the road, such a monumental milestone to maturity, this thing called marriage! And it all starts with a wedding.

It doesn't have to be a fancy one, or big for that matter. But it does have to *be*. No, not other than in narrative fashion do we actually find the Word of God instructing us about weddings. Rather, it instructs us about life and marriage and children being born and parented and about finances and human sexuality, roles in relationships, and priorities, and from it ALL we learn something perhaps about what a wedding should look like.

In keeping with the current tradition, and for practical purposes, we had a rehearsal the night before the wedding. Three of Rachel's sisters and their husbands and three of my brothers and their wives would provide the six witnesses for the ceremony. Her pastor would officiate the marriage vows, and the youth pastor from my home church would provide a devotional. Lester Troyer, a respected instructor from Maranatha Bible School, would deliver the sermon. Eight of our mutual friends and family members would sing worship songs in a cappella harmony. Both of our fathers would offer benedictory prayers. We practiced both the processional and the recessional several times, gathered in a quick huddle for last-minute reminders, and then retreated to the church dining hall in the basement for the rehearsal dinner.

Wow! I wish Rachel were here to fill in all the beautiful details that mattered so much to her about our wedding day: dresses for the bridesmaids, waitresses, and other attendants, color schemes, table and seating arrangements, flower vases, and all. I had spun out the wooden vases on a lathe several weeks before, and I know there were no two exactly alike. This she proclaimed was just as it should be since no two people are alike, and these were her unique gifts to all our friends and family who helped us that day. She designed and arranged the silk flowers for the vases and this much I know—they were beautiful, both the vases I had made and the flowers she had arranged. Years later, as we visited friends and family from around the country, we'd see those vases and flowers sitting on fireplace mantels, bedroom dressers, and other creative places throughout their homes.

The day went by so fast. Rachel was absolutely adorable in her pure white wedding dress. Even now, looking back upon the pictures taken nearly thirty years ago, I can see the radiance of her joy. She was surrounded by her family. Three out of four grandparents were there that day. They meant the world to her! Her parents were there—something only one out of our five children will be able to say on their wedding days, now that their mother is missing. Her brothers and sisters, uncles and aunts, and cousins were there. And friends from all over. And I was there!

As the initiator in our relationship, it meant so much to me to see how much joy she found in this day. We were both old enough and mature enough to know that many challenges in marriage lay ahead, but that didn't subtract at all from the pure joy of this day. We had found in each other a love from God for us to share. We sensed His call, not only on our lives individually, but now on our marriage as well. We knew it was about something bigger than ourselves. It was really all about Him, and we were honored to be called to illustrate the relationship He, the God of the universe, longs to have with each of His created ones and the relationship He the Bridegroom longs to have with His Bride, the church. This we knew was really what marriage was to portray, and this is what we wanted our wedding to imagine as well. Such depths of reality stirred us profoundly that day!

The songs rang out the joy of that message: "Always cheerful, always cheerful! Sunshine all around we see. Full of beauty is the path of duty. Cheerful we will always be!" The wedding sermon detailed the absolute honor the Bride of Christ bestows upon her Bridegroom and the wonderful delight the Bridegroom ravishes upon His Bride. Love and respect; honor and cherishing care; victory, reverence, and worship for our good and awesome and wonderful God—these were the themes of the day.

My bride and I.

Reflections in Marriage

3. The Importance of Cleaving (Bride)

<u>The Real Thing</u>:

The church must cleave to Christ. To the perfectly faithful church at Smyrna: " ...be thou faithful unto death, and I will give thee a crown of life" (Rev. 2:10b).

Only those who are part of the cleaving, faithful church will receive a reward.

<u>The Reflection</u>:

Wives must be "glued" faithfully to their husbands with the same inseparable bond as their husbands are to them. "Let not the wife depart from her husband: But if she depart, let her remain unmarried, or be reconciled to her husband" (1 Cor. 7:10-11).

"How-tos" For Couples

Her HAPPINESS—The MYSTERY!

I've just listed seven secrets of what it took to make Rachel happy as my wife. But there's really an eighth one too. In fact, it's more than a secret; it's a mystery. Did you know wives are mysterious? There's something unique about every wife and her relationship with herself, her husband, and her happiness that remains a mystery even they cannot define. But they love it when you discover it!

R _elationship____ Husbands: More than she loves you, she loves this.
C _onnection____ Talk about yourself or don't bother getting married!
O _penness_____ She is body modest, but soul naked.
C _hildren_____ Give her as many of these as her heart desires.
C _onversation___ Tender words, gentle touch, and a good ...
F _riends_____ Share these: What's hers is yours.
F _amily_____ This comes along with the marriage.
M _ystery_____ The wonder of it all!

This, by the way, is totally biblical. In Ephesians 5, where we find the Apostle Paul's primary treatise about marriage, he calls it a mystery. He then explains that he's speaking concerning Christ and the church—the Bride of Christ. And the format he uses is that God designed marriage from the beginning of time to be a beautiful picture of the relationship He (the bridegroom) wants to have with you (His bride).

I know some Christians who are so beautiful, so true to this bride/bridegroom image that I really believe if the whole world could know them, the whole world would accept Christ as their bridegroom too. So if you are a believer in Christ and have a heart for evangelism at all, the first thing you should consider is marriage. "Wait a minute!" you say. "I'd love to get married, but I've always been overlooked as a potential bride, or rejected as a potential bridegroom. You just can't make such a sweeping statement!" Well? Christ has been rejected by many brides He would consider darling to have. And the church has been overlooked and even ignored by many who should be modeling the bridegroom of Christ within her. Yet Christ being rejected doesn't keep Him from still BEING who He is as the perfect Bridegroom, and the fact that the church is overlooked, ignored, and even derided doesn't keep her from BEING who she is as the bride of Christ who will one day be taken home to His heaven to enjoy total intimacy with Him forever.

There was something about Rachel's happiness that always remained a mystery to me. About the time I'd think I discovered it, or was finally able to quantify it or define its quality, *poof!*—it was gone! She still loved our relationship, when it was what it needed to be. She still reveled in heartfelt connection. She still loved to hang her heart wide open upon my listening ear. She still loved her children dearly, still longed for conversation, and still treasured her friends and family enormously. But the mystery still existed. When it revealed itself, she was elated, but when it was not discovered, she was tempted to deflation. She really couldn't describe it, and it's for sure that if she couldn't describe it, I was completely dumfounded to define it for her.

I love you today because … you are a promise keeper.

To this day, the closest I can get to explaining it is simply in the pursuit. When I was forever pursuing her heart, she was forever happy. When I was distracted, her happiness subsided. When I was preoccupied, her happiness lay dormant. But when she knew that I at least had her on my mind, we were getting close.

Sound mysterious? It was! But it's beautiful because it pictures our delight when we fully discover how desperately in love with us God is. Most Christians are unhappy because they don't realize this. And most wives are unhappy because they don't realize it either—either because it's just not there from their husbands, or like the Bride of Christ, the church, they are simply not basking in the love. For Rachel and I, it was a bit of both. And it remained a mystery, for we could only see through a glass darkly, not yet face to face. Rachel now embraces that perfect experience in heaven! On earth, I still embrace the mystery.

CHAPTER 10

Season of Honeymoons

Rachel's Story

That first two-hour leg of our honeymoon trip, driving from Freeport to Chicago, is forever riveted in my memory. It'd been the quickest day of our lives—our wedding and then quickly back to the farmhouse where she'd grown up. In the corner of her upstairs bedroom, we'd shared our first kiss. Now sitting as close together as we could possibly get in my brother's Chevy Luv pickup with our arms around each other, I still managed to drive despite head-to-toe sensations I'd never felt before. We spent Sunday there in Chicago, even managing to make it to church that day for an evening service.

But wow! Back to that first night! I'd determined long before that I wasn't going to make sex the center of everything on the first night. But we might as well have done so! I don't think either of us got a wink of sleep and the hilarity of what we did get would keep us in stitches every time we recounted it together for the next twenty-eight years. Enough said.

Ann Arbor, Michigan, was our next stop, and then across the Canadian border to Windsor, Ontario, the next night and on to Niagara Falls by Wednesday. Thursday evening found us all the way to the New England states where we had a honeymoon suite reserved for four days in New Hampshire. It was in that honeymoon suite where we experienced our first minor misunderstanding in marriage.

We had made a great little meal together that evening and then sat down at the rustic wooden table to eat and gaze into each other's eyes. Those deep, dark eyes pulled me toward her every time. The next thing I knew I was dragging her toward the couch so I could see them even better. But Rachel, being the more responsible one between us, wanted to clear off the table first before relaxing. In our super sensitive honeymoon sensations, I took it personal that she was putting the dishes first, and she took it personal that I took it personal. We made up over the dishes when

I offered that we just wash them up and get them all done while we were at it. Then we finally headed for the couch, doing a three-minute sideways two-step which left us both panting for air. As we sat down together, I scooted over a bit, and she thought I was trying to get away from her. But I just needed to catch my breath.

Pulling her over, I looked into those beautiful eyes and said, "You make me crazy!"

"No, I'm crazy for you," she retorted as we folded ourselves together and spent the sixth night of our marriage on the couch.

Well, we made it through that evening with a few lessons in hand and went on to have three more wonderful days in the gorgeous, fall-colored White Mountains of New Hampshire. There would be many more adjustments we'd make throughout the next twenty-eight years of marriage, but those very first ones are the most memorable. While I've accepted the loss of Rachel, I find myself wishing I could still be making adjustments with her. There's something about a lifetime of melding two lives together that's kind of addicting. I just have an insatiable thirst for more!

Coming home from our honeymoon on the states side, we stopped in Ohio, where I looked up an old friend, Dennis Langer, who was attending Kent State University at the time. I'd worked with Dennis on a construction crew in Phoenix, and we'd had many conversations about the Lord. He was clearly a skeptic, but an honest one, and I wanted to maintain as much contact with him as possible. That stop would be Rachel's first experience with ministry getting in the way of marriage, but it certainly wouldn't be the last.

She took it well and patiently waited in the Luv while I went into the ten-story library building to see if I could find Dennis. (Of course, this was before the days of cell phones or he could have guided me right in to where he was sitting.) After searching several floors, I finally found him on the seventh level, sitting in a study booth. I nearly walked right passed him, and the bugle eyes he gave me when he unexpectedly saw me standing there was worth it all. I was the last person he was expecting to walk up to him on the seventh floor of the library building at Kent State University. Within an hour I was back to loving my bride in the Chevy Luv.

In less than two weeks we were back in Illinois settling into our little one-bedroom apartment attached to Grandpa and Grandma Graybill's house in Dakota. We had $6.00 left in our pocket (besides what we had been given as gifts on our wedding day), but the apartment came completely furnished including a single bed for the bedroom. (That, by the way, is how we got our firstborn so fast.) Eventually we spent our wedding gift money on a queen size water bed, which took us well into the eighteenth year of our marriage. After that we got a dual controlled air mattress, which I still have to this day.

In January 1985, ten weeks into our marriage, we embarked upon another honeymoon experience—our first term serving as deans of men and women at Maranatha Bible School. Those were fun months, bridging the gap between young people and staff in an environment of worship and learning. Directing the choir with Rachel singing in it and teaching one class besides was a lot of fun. I'll never forget the night we both sat straight up in bed as we heard the snowy crunch of footsteps on the flat roof overhead. Sure enough, the next morning when I climbed up to check things out, there were footsteps going the entire length of the school building roof and then the intruder had jumped off the other end into a snowbank. I came away quite certain it wasn't any of the students but some town fellow who decided to take a midnight winter hike on the roof of a Bible school.

Another first for us was to teach in tandem at the Kitchi Pines School where Rachel had been teaching when we first started dating. To her, it was like coming home. She always loved the Kitchi church environment and had taught in the church school for a total of six years before. Now to be doing so together was a treat for both of us. Her years of teaching are a lot of what made her into the awesome mother and homeschool teacher to our own children in the years following.

A couple of months short of our sixth wedding anniversary, I was ordained by the Midwest Fellowship as an assistant pastor at Northwood Chapel near Littlefork, Minnesota. While this, too, was a first for us, there was no honeymoon! Out of a sense of desperation from having his son suddenly resign as pastor, our overseer had immediately arranged for an ordination to replace him within six months. The church was still reeling from the domestic infighting of the overseer's family, and a novice brother was campaigning hard to be his replacement. So when I was chosen by the church to be ordained, it came with an entire package of unresolved issues. This was the context in which Rachel would develop her first several points of her list "Why I Hate Being a Pastor's Wife."

While this experience launched us into the realm of church leadership, ministry, and pastoral care like nothing else could have, it came close to destroying us at the same time. I remember Howard Bean, the conference moderator for the Midwest Fellowship, quoting someone else at the time of our introduction to the conference, saying that to ordain someone to the ministry is to "lessen their chances for heaven." I've come to believe that much of what we'd assumed personal responsibility for was nothing less than direct spiritual warfare with all of Satan's forces set against us. These were all positions we were called to by God in one way or another. Perhaps we could have refused them and maybe even should have. But God gave us peace at each turning point, and in retrospect, while I wouldn't want to do it all over again, I wouldn't change a thing. The life-shaping, door-opening lessons were invaluable to us both, and it provided a crucible of grace for our children too. Did they suffer? Certainly, right along with me and Rachel. But the life-skills these experiences honed for our family could never have been mastered any other way. God knows what He's about!

There were times it felt like that was precisely the intended goal on the part of some who played political hardball with our lives: to send us straight to hell. But without the ordination at Northwood Chapel, I doubt that I'd ever have had the courage to be part of starting Christian Life Chapel in International Falls seven years later. And without the ten years' experience at CLC, it's hard to imagine having the courage to follow the Lord all the way to Los Angeles. And without these seven years here already, I'd never be ready for the current threshold of church planting ministry now. One thing leads to another, grace upon grace upon grace, with open doors abounding everywhere.

The Only Safe Place to Be

Rachel was a cautious, quiet homebody. Doing new things was not necessarily her first forte. But, for a pioneer like me, she was the perfect partner. Without her on many of these frontiers, I would have probably been wiped out on the first foray. She kept me grounded and real, yet she was always ready to follow me as I followed Christ. That's why I kept calling her "Honeybunch": a bunch of reality and always sweet 'n sticky, sticking with me through thick and thin.

Coming to Los Angeles was her last "honeymoon" experience with me. She struggled to think of living within such a huge metropolis. I remember saying rather prophetically to her one time when we were processing the whole thing of moving to L.A.: "I think God has a little home for you right in the middle of Los Angeles, someplace where you'll feel perfectly comfortable and safe." I didn't say it to twist her arm, but I said it simply because I felt like I should say it. And at the time, it was amazing to me how she accepted it as almost a promise.

Twenty months later, after starting out temporarily in the Inland Empire, we were regularly touring rental homes within L.A. proper in anticipation of the move we'd need to make when our Upland rental contract expired on October 1, 2009. Rather than needlessly dragging everyone through a bunch of houses, I looked at over 50 homes myself in a prescreening process to weed out anything I knew right off would not be suitable for our family. Then, if I thought one carried some possibility, I'd bring Rachel along with as many of the children as possible. We toured several dozen homes that way. Each time, I could tell almost without a word whether this was the one or not. There were a couple houses that felt pretty good to everyone, but then for some reason or other, they would fall through or someone else would beat us to the deal.

But just in the nick of time a home popped up on the online Westside Rental site we had subscribed to. It was in the Mt. Washington area. I drove past and thought it looked promising. The only thing I worried about was that it was located along a pretty steep street, and we'd all agreed as a family that we didn't want to live on the side of a hill. But it was worth a try. So I picked up Rachel one day and we went to look at the house. It had five bedrooms, which was nice so we could accommodate our VSers when they came. Even though four of the five bedrooms were pretty small, the master bedroom was good sized and had its own bathroom. It was a tri-level home with the kitchen, living room, and dining rooms all on the main middle level. Two bedrooms were on the lower level with another bathroom, a family room, lots of storage space, and an office area besides. The other three bedrooms including the master were on the upper floor with another full bathroom. We walked through the home several times. I could tell Rachel was getting into this one.

As we left the house and walked back down the six percent slope to our car, I turned and asked her, "So what do you think?"

Her response immediately took me back to the prophetic statement I'd made to her 20 months earlier. She smiled that knowingly crooked little grin and said simply, "There isn't anything wrong with this one!"

I knew then and there we had nailed it; she would feel safe and secure in this home. It wasn't right in the middle of Los Angeles as I had suggested, but it would be right in the center of God's will. And that's the only safe place to be!

Her Inspiration

About this same time, during our musings and discussions back in Minnesota as we worked out our response to Choice Books' invitation to move to Los Angeles, one day Rachel said to me, "If we move to Los Angeles, do you know what I'd really enjoy?"

"No, what's that?" I replied, eagerly wanting to accumulate in my heart and mind all of the things that would make her the happiest with such a momentous move across the country.

"If I could learn to know a friendly black lady there somewhere, and we could sit and have tea once in a while … I think that would be so sweet."

On the Friday before her death, just minutes before we crawled into our 2003 Kia minivan before heading out for Asher's wedding in Colorado, Rachel said, "I wonder if Dashiel would take care of Caspian and Tinker for us while we're gone. She seems to like animals."

Caspian and Tinker are our dog and cat. But Dashiel is our neighbor lady right across the street from us where she lives with her husband Mike and their two kids. Dashiel is originally from England. Rachel just loved her lilting English accent and would often say, "I'd really like to learn to know her better sometime!" Because of the fondness and frequency with which she'd say this, I was beginning to wonder if perhaps Dashiel was the "black lady" Rachel had been hoping to learn to know so she could have tea with her once in a while.

"I don't know," I replied. "Perhaps she would enjoy that—oh, look! She's just outside their house right now. Why don't you go ask her?"

"No, I don't want to bother her right now. She looks like she's busy," Rachel reasoned, sounding kind of discouraged.

"No. Seriously! Why don't you go find out?" I urged.

"Ok, I'll be right back," she said as she hurried across the street.

I went ahead and got into the van as I waited for her to return. A couple minutes later she came back, all enthused.

"I'm so excited!" she exclaimed, her face aglow. "She'll do it for us. And now I have her phone number, her cell number, and even her email address. I'm really looking forward to learning to know her better when we get back from the wedding."

But she never got back. Four days later she went to heaven instead where there are many wonderful ladies to have celestial tea with, both English ladies and black ladies too.

In recent months I've reflected back upon Rachel's love for tea (for conversation really), her love for heart-to-heart connection, and her desire to one day have regular tea and conversation with a friendly black lady. I think she would really enjoy Akua (ah-kwee-ah) Osei-bonsu, a lady from Ghana who's been attending our fellowship in recent months. I can just imagine the two of them enjoying each other over a cup of Akua's honey-ginger tea and praying together. Rachel was a private prayer warrior, aligning herself with the Lord and doing battle with the enemy from her home and prayer closet, yet she was willing also to pray publicly with me around the flagpole on the city square in International Falls. Akua is a passionate prayer warrior who also aligns herself with the Lord and does hand-to-hand conflict with the enemy from her television program, a more public platform for prayer. But she is also willing to lock herself in her bedroom for eight to ten hours at a time, praying privately and interceding for countless of her friends and family. Somehow I think they'd probably be friends, have tea, and pray together.

The Bride of Christ

There are honeymoon stages for the church too. The Acts of the Apostles record many awesome first-time experiences for the newly founded church Jesus established here on earth in the short three and a half years of His life's ministry.

Imagine experiencing that first outpouring of the Holy Spirit on the day of Pentecost. The thrill of divine influence, of seeing God meet man in a way never before encountered. What would it have been like to watch Christ's ascension back into heaven and to hear His voice, "You will receive power when the Holy Spirit comes upon you" (Acts 1:8)?

Inherent power, power for performing miracles, moral power, the power of influence, the power of numbers—all this power was given for the first time by the Holy Spirit to the church. What a thrilling honeymoon!

Imagine watching 3,000 people get saved at one time! Imagine the impact of such an event in one city. It was the first time ever! What would it have been like to be part of the formation of that first fellowship? Witnessing the first supernatural healings by the apostles? Hearing those first sermons and the debates between those first church leaders and the fledgling church taking on the established Jewish system? Christians hauled before a court of law and found guilty of preaching Jesus for the first time in history? Or what it would have been like to sell everything you had, pool all your resources, and share everything in common? And wow! What about that Ananias and Sapphira ordeal?

The Jerusalem conference—now that was a real honeymoon trying to hammer out a fix for the differences between Jewish and Gentile believers and then seeing the unity that came out of that first collection of insight and wisdom in an effort to resolve a practical church problem. What would it have been like to have been one of those first seven deacons? Or what would it have been like to watch your deacon stoned to death in the public square? How would it have affected your faith to experience the sudden breakup of the church as everyone fled for their lives? Would you have liked to be around when this Saul guy of Tarsus first showed up? And then to witness his whole transformation, converting from persecutor to persecuted?

And what of the challenge of trying to incorporate Gentile people into a body of Jewish believers? What must it have been like for Peter to explain his vision of a weird sheet full of unclean animals that they could now eat and needing to convince everyone that this was indeed from the Lord and not just his own imagination running overtime? And then Peter's receiving that "get out of jail free" card as he was miraculously led out of prison. I'd have loved to have heard him tell that story to everyone else!

And then Paul started taking those extended missionary journeys and reporting back about all the excitement—and opposition—throughout the region. The squabble that broke out between Paul and Barnabas was so great they couldn't work together anymore. Would that have been the first church split? Then there was that huge outbreak in Ephesus—what a riot! It sure was a silly plan for how to kill Paul, and wouldn't it have been neat to have been a part of helping him avoid it? And those amazing appearances Paul had before Felix, Festus, Agrippa—what a racket that was! He was such a great mentor for everyone. Plus the shipwreck he had and poisonous snake bite he miraculously survived. What a guy! What a God he had! And what a honeymoon as the early church was established!

Reflections in Marriage

4. The Love/Respect Factor (Bridegroom)

THE REAL THING:

Christ loved His Bride the church enough to die for her.

"Even as Christ also loved the church and gave himself for it" (Eph. 5:25b).

THE REFLECTION:

Husbands must be sacrificial lovers.

"Husbands, love your wives, even as Christ also loved the church and gave himself for it" (Eph. 5:25).

Real love is measured by sacrifice. The divine and spiritual authority of a husband must be rooted in the sacrifice of himself. True love is accompanied by humility. Headship is not a right; it is a duty! Such humility typifies the kind that was demonstrated by Christ.

"<u>Have this attitude in yourselves</u> which was also in Christ Jesus, who, although He existed in the form of God, did not regard equality with God a thing to be grasped, but **emptied Himself**, taking the form of a bondservant, and being made in the likeness of men. And being found in appearance as a man, he humbled Himself by becoming obedient <u>to the point of death</u>, even death on a cross" (Phil. 2:5-8, NASB).

"How-tos" For Couples

She Honored My Relationships

For women, it's about HAPPINESS ... a cheerfulness that comes from feeling fully cherished as the unique treasure God made them to be. For men, it's about HONOR ... a sense of significance that comes from feeling fully recognized for the distinctive value God has invested in them.

This is not academic. It's instinctive. It's heart stuff for both men and women. For me to connect with Rachel's heart, I needed to care about her happiness. And for her to connect with mine, she needed to care about my honor. Some men just don't get it and couldn't care less about their wives' happiness, and some women are just as clueless about honor, dismissing it as an ego trip for men.

Seven secrets, yea eight, if you count the mystery of it all, were the keys to Rachel's happiness that were connected directly to her heart. Six of these tied right to my heart, as well, revealing how she honored me as her husband.

R = ___Relationships___: Face to face in marriage; shoulder to shoulder with my friends.

A = _____: The desire to serve and to lead is the essence of authority and manhood.

C = _____: God has put within every male image-bearer of Himself this chromosome.

H = _____: Something within the genes of a man longs to provide for and protect those under his care.

E = _____: Many women are shame-based in their approach to men. But this is the opposite of shame.

L = _____: This is powerful to a man. An honoring woman believes in her man more than he believes in himself.

Not only did relationships matter to Rachel for herself, but they mattered to her for me as well. First of all, she wanted to give me the value of a deep marriage relationship. So as my wife, she cared about my heart, even at times when I tended to neglect it myself. She was intent on discovering what it was that made me come alive as a person spiritually, emotionally, and physically. She knew that if our marriage was going to be good, it would need to thrive on each of these levels.

Rachel cared about my relationship with the Lord and was a constant support to me spiritually, making sure I always had adequate time alone with Him. She also cared about my spiritual gifts and loved to see them in action. She honored my emotions as well. She got my sense of humor and rallied to my joy, but she also understood that when a man's emotions are hurt he tends to get angry, in contrast to a woman who will cry.

Rachel wanted my relationship with her to be complete, so she gave herself to me in every way: spirit, soul, and body. She subscribed to the simple doctrine put forward by Paul in the Scriptures and emphasized by Dr. Laura and Sarah Eggerichs who ask their female audiences, "Why would you ever deny him something that takes so little time and makes him so happy?" Or, I might say, " …that makes him feel so honored!?" To have sex with the most beautiful woman in the world is an honor any wife can give her man!

But Rachel didn't just honor my relationship with HER—she saw all of my friendships as important. She respected my need for shoulder-to-shoulder connections with other men. She loved my coffee times and prayer meetings with Christian men in our community and saw the need for building redemptive relationships as crucial to evangelism among unbelievers. And while sometimes she felt neglected by me, she didn't often resent ME for it. Rather, she worked to maintain positive attitudes toward the crowds and circumstances that pulled me away from her so many times. But the fact that other people loved me, too, only made her admire me more.

To all of you women who long for deeper intimacy with your man—take this tip from Rachel's life as a woman of influence. Your husband is going to remember the keys to your happiness if you'll remember to honor his heart too. He's a man, so don't approach your relationship to him in the same way you would your lady friends. Let him be who he is: your male counterpart. And give him the time, space, and support to rumble with other men too! In the meantime, go have tea with your girlfriends.

CHAPTER 11

No End to Beauty—This Bride

Rachel's Story

Many wonderful women never marry. But when Rachel and I were married in 1984, seventy percent of American women married before 24 years of age. So, statistically for her to have been 28 years old when we married was outside of the expected averages. This in itself stretched her confidence in God's ability to provide for her, and it exercised her faith in ways that would prove to be not only of benefit to her back then, but also in counseling and encouraging many other young women along the way in the years since. Women who not only survive this trial of faith but THRIVE in the experience are women worth noting. And, I'll hasten to add—they are women worth marrying!

But the wait can be demoralizing. However, the bigger danger and indictment lies with the MEN who SHOULD be marrying them. Even Christian men so often consider the qualities of character and inner beauty to be way too far down the list. No wonder more than fifty percent of "Christian" marriages end in divorce, right in line with the percentages for unbelievers.

Rachel had several suitors before I came along. One of them thought she was too "forward." Can you imagine that? Not if you really knew Rachel! She wasn't forward at all—he was just plain backward! Another one thought she was too quiet. Now how about that? Especially after having just come away from being called "forward." Would to God more people would simply shut up when they have nothing to say! And then there was that other guy who coaxed a kiss out of her and then promptly broke up with her. He carried the qualities of a first class jerk! But that's ok. She escaped the tragedy of ever being married to him and ever needing to kiss him again. And as for me—no, she was not too forward and she was not too quiet. She was just right! And the kiss? Well, I can take you right to the spot where we had our first kiss, up there in the corner of her bedroom on the evening of our wedding day, AFTER the wedding, just before we headed for Chicago to spend our first night together.

Those were some of the rigors of Rachel's early adult life. But there were still other rigors to come. Being married to me was in itself no small feat. Everything you need to know about Rachel can be summed up in the profound way in which she was "meet [suitable] for him" (Gen. 2:18). She allowed herself to be "formed around my rib" in such a way that brought her strengths to complement my weaknesses so perfectly. This was true both in the typical male/female differences of cerebral/strength/leadership versus the heart/support/relationship characteristics.

But perhaps even more significant was the remarkable agility with which she balanced me out in our areas of personal differences. I was outgoing and talkative; she was reserved and thoughtful. I was adventurous and a bit of a risk-taker; she loved the familiar paths and was eternally careful. (This is why I ache inside every time I wonder how it could be that she pulled out in front of that Dodge Ram pickup truck the day she died. It was so unlike her!) I loved public places, but for her, our home was her haven. In short, she was the making of me. She was my perfect counterpart.

Rachel followed me everywhere the Lord led us. But she was not a pushover. Instead she was strong with a clear sense of overall direction. Yet she followed me! She would leave the quiet contentment of our home time and again and go out into public places to connect with people she'd never met, just because she knew it meant so much to me to have her along.

Just two years after our marriage, she left the placid farmland of northern Illinois to follow me into the recreational borderland community of Voyager's National Park and the "Icebox of the Nation"—International Falls, Minnesota. And then twenty-one years later she followed me again, not back home to the safe and familiar, but into the "uttermost parts" of inner city Los Angeles. I know beyond the shadow of a doubt that if it were not for her determination to honor me as her husband and to trust God in my ability to hear from Him, there is no way she would have made the move. WHO Rachel was did not fit naturally with WHAT Los Angeles is. But move she did! And that to my wonderful delight and the bountiful blessing of every life she touched in the four years and seven months she would be there before her death.

Her Inspiration

Rachel loved a good laugh! Whether it was her own keen sense of humor, or coming from her boys or her brothers, and even sometimes from yours truly, she loved to laugh. Her brothers especially had some rather comical strains that were particularly endearing to her, which her boys promptly picked up on through an almost osmotic effect from regular exposure.

The email below illustrates one particular strain. The mix of nearly painful nostalgia and pleasant amusement picked her up a bit and plucked her from this melancholy moment.

She writes to her siblings and parents about how the silence seems so loud with her sixteen-year-old son Asher flying half a world away on a visit to Thailand, sensing Marcel and Krista's relationship getting serious, and Carita finishing up her degree in English—all giving her that foreboding feeling that parents get when their children leave the nest. She ends it with a reference to the cat wandering through the house, meowing. Her brother Dan picks up on it and likens himself to the cat meowing, which Carita then collaborates with concerning the sentence structure and, of course, her degree in English. So then Rachel offers to come help her brother figure out what he'd need to stop wandering through the house meowing and then says she's glad **she's** not wandering around the house meowing. Enjoy the exchange!

---------- Forwarded Message ----------
From: Rachel Witmer rhwitmer@hotmail.com
Subject: RE: The silence is so loud today …
Date: Tue, 19 Apr 2011 12:16:44 –0500
Should I come figure out what you need? Carita thought it sounded like *I* was wandering through the house, meowing … that's not happening … yet anyway!

----- Forwarded Message -----
From: Dan Schrader, dps1831@comcast.net
Subject: Re: The silence is so loud today …
Date: Tue, 19 Apr 2011 10:45:19 –0500
I can relate … to the cat.

----- Original Message -----
From: Rachel Witmer rhwitmer@hotmail.com
Sent: Monday, April 18, 2011 4:01 PM
Subject: The silence is so loud today …

This morning, we took Asher and his good friend, Duane, to the airport. Their Moms are glad they can travel together. They should be in the air now for their 14-hour flight to Chang Hai, China, where they have a 17 1/2 hour layover and then to KunMing in China for a 26-hour layover before their last flight to Chang Mai, Thailand, arriving sometime on Thursday.

It was a bit harder to see him go, in part because there could be a number of major changes in the coming months and family life "may never be quite like today." Carita is working on finishing up her course of study in the next few months and then what? Kristi is finishing school and hoping to go to SMBI next winter and if Marcel and Krista keep going as they are, he is talking of spending his winter break in PA and/or moving out there for a while after school next year. But we train them to follow God and there comes a time to let them go … and 'give' them back, so to speak … free to follow. I thank God for all the wonderful memories … and more that will come in a different sort of way!

Today besides Marcel and Asher being gone, Carita is at work and Kristi and Christopher just left with Ernest to go over to the warehouse. They are going to be doing some of Asher's jobs with the books while he is gone.

So here I am, trying to figure out what is wrong with the cat … wandering through the house meowing … hmmm.

God bless you all!

Love,
Rachel

The Bride of Christ

Just like the first bride Eve was so easily dissuaded from God in the beautiful Garden of Eden under Adam's doting eye, so we as Christians can get so quickly distracted from Christ even though He has provided us with everything we need to succeed. The Apostle Peter pleads with us:

"Grace and peace be multiplied unto you through the knowledge of God, and of Jesus our Lord, According as his divine power hath given unto us all things that pertain unto life and godliness, through the knowledge of him that hath called us to glory and virtue: Whereby are given unto us exceeding great and precious promises: that by these ye might be partakers of the divine nature, having escaped the corruption that is in the world through lust.

"And beside this, giving all diligence, add to your faith virtue; and to virtue knowledge; And to knowledge temperance; and to temperance patience; and to patience godliness; And to godliness brotherly kindness; and to brotherly kindness charity. For if these things be in you, and abound, they make you that ye shall neither be barren nor unfruitful in the knowledge of our Lord Jesus Christ. But he that lacketh these things is blind, and cannot see afar off, and hath forgotten that he was purged from his old sins.

"Wherefore the rather, brethren, give diligence to make your calling and election sure: for if ye do these things, ye shall never fall: For so an entrance shall be ministered unto you abundantly into the everlasting kingdom of our Lord and Saviour Jesus Christ" (2 Peter 1:2-11).

The things that make a bride so beautiful and sweet also make her vulnerable in other ways. So it is with the Bride of Christ. To become His bride means to expose ourselves to Him in every way ... to become totally vulnerable and at His disposal. It's a volatile relationship—all or none, now or never. He calls us to Himself but makes no promise that He'll keep calling if we harden our hearts. The writer of Hebrews says, "Today is the day of salvation. Today if you hear His voice, do not harden your hearts."

And Paul, in 1 Corinthians 11:3, says, "For I am jealous over you with godly jealousy: for I have espoused you to one husband, that I may present you as a chaste virgin to Christ. But I fear, lest by any means, as the serpent beguiled Eve through his subtilty, so your minds should be corrupted from the simplicity that is in Christ."

He was afraid that the Corinthian church was going to go off and have an affair with the world or with other religions that were vying for its affections. He had officiated in their marriage to Christ, but now they were flirting around and entertaining ideas about others. They were being deceived by the enticing words of those who were promising them the world. Such folks were claiming to be "ministers of righteousness" but were actually the ministers of Satan.

Many things flirt for our attention in the church today too. On the right hand are ideas and philosophies that sound safe and secure but in reality only get us to trust in false securities like a harlot promises love, but once she has your money, that's all she ever really wanted. On the left hand are the vain enticements of sensual things that only satisfy the flesh and ego and are just as transient as the other.

But God wants us, pure and simple! All of us. For good. He wants a marriage, not the fling of the next best thing. He is our Bridegroom! And His jealousy is all about our good, for His glory. Let's be faithful to Him until death when we get to fall into His loving arms forever.

Reflections in Marriage

4. The Love/Respect Factor (Bride)

THE REAL THING:

The real church always honors Christ, her Bridegroom.

"Therefore, as the church is subject unto Christ ..." (Eph. 5:24a).

THE REFLECTION:

Wives should always be respectful to their husbands.

"...and the wife see that she respect [reverence–KJV] her husband" (Eph. 5:33).

In the same way the church always honors Christ, so wives should respect their husbands.

"Therefore <u>as the church is subject unto Christ</u>, so let the wives be to their own husbands <u>in every thing</u>" (Eph. 5:24).

Respect is really a mutual condition, and a loving husband certainly offers freedom of expression, but then it becomes her responsibility to support him and honor him for what God has called him to be and do. This does not suggest inequality. Christ was submissive, too, but still equal with, the Father.

"I and my Father are one" (Jn. 10:30).

"...he that hath seen me hath seen the Father" (Jn. 14:9b).

There is great purpose in submission. Wives need not chafe in submission, because they are typifying an eternal substance by living according to divine order.

"How-tos" For Couples

She Honored Me for My Authority

Consider how the "A" equaled "Authority" in Rachel's honor for me.

R = ___Relationships___: Face to face in marriage; shoulder to shoulder with my friends.

A = ___Authority___: The desire to serve and to lead is the essence of authority and manhood.

C = _____: God has put within every male image-bearer of Himself this chromosome.

H = _____: Something within the genes of a man longs to provide for and protect those under his care.

E = _____: Many women are shame-based in their approach to men. But this is the opposite of shame.

L = _____: This is powerful to a man. An honoring woman believes in her man more than he believes in himself.

Remember: For women, I'm suggesting it's all about HAPPINESS—a cheerfulness born from feeling fully cherished as the unique treasure God made them to be. But for men, it's about HONOR—that sense of significance which comes from feeling fully recognized for the distinctive value God has invested in them. Again, it's not an academic thing. Instead it's instinctive. It's heart stuff for both men and women. For me to connect with Rachel's heart, I needed to care about her happiness; for her to connect with mine, she cared about my honor. I feel sorry for the wives of men who just don't get it and are careless about their wives' happiness. My heart also goes out to the men who are married to women who are just as clueless about honor, dismissing out-of-hand the hearts of their husbands as egomaniac.

Seven secrets revealed the keys to Rachel's happiness, eight counting the element of mystery. These keys opened directly to her heart. At the same time there were six particular things that tied directly to my heart and were revealing of how she honored me as her husband.

Rachel honored my desire to serve and to lead, which is the real essence of authority. If anything, sometimes it seemed to me that she saw me as the authority on everything. Sometimes I had to convince her I didn't feel like I was an authority about this or that. And she was usually amazed and disbelieving about it. But you can imagine how honored this usually made me feel as her man!

She wanted a leader. She wanted someone ahead of her, someone willing to take responsibility, not only for himself, but for her too. She wanted a head. She felt secure and protected in this. She felt loved.

You see, authority is not about being boss, and it's certainly not about being better or more important. It's a creation thing. Adam was first created, and then Eve. God made Adam at such a time and in such a way in order to plan and prepare and get things ready for others who would follow. God gave Adam responsibilities he didn't give Eve. He gave her other responsibilities. It's not a matter of equality. In spite of what Abraham Lincoln said, not even two men are created equal nor are two women. Both are unique. But it's a matter of roles and responsibilities in particular.

Because of my "falleness," having died in Adam, I haven't always functioned to my fullest. This was frustrating to Rachel, but she still chose to honor me. And because Eve was deceived, so also was Rachel at times, which caused her to worry, occasionally to nag, and even sometimes take over. But we both knew God's design for marriage and so much enjoyed the mutual fulfillment we found in His ways, that we could never stray far from the pattern for long.

Authority is the power of initiation, thinking ahead, dreaming, spawning new life. Ever wonder why only women can become pregnant and only men impregnate? Men move in; women rally 'round. It's the complement interplay between initiation and response. It really only works in loving relationships, but when it does, it's powerful!

Now Rachel wasn't like some women who HAVE to have the most important or most powerful husband around in order for them to feel fulfilled. She found it silly to waste time with such competition. She didn't really care about how I measured up to other men. What mattered to her was US, and she absolutely honored my role as the authority figure in her life.

CHAPTER 12

The Mother Bride

Rachel's Story

Firstborn in her family, a matriarch of teachers, the spiritual gift of discernment—nothing could have qualified Rachel more as a mother. There were other roles she shunned and other capacities she was not called to, but mothering was her passion. Would she have been as good a mother at nineteen or even twenty-one? Who knows? But I highly doubt it. Sure, she could have become just as pregnant, perhaps she could have even nursed as well, or even better, changed pampers equally, cooed smiles out of babies, and coached toddlers along. But the sheer discipline of delayed marriage, added years of service to others, and experiential knowledge of life in general qualified her as little else could have. She was an absolutely awesome wife, but if it's possible, she was an even better mother. She cherished her daughters and admired her sons. She was many things to many people, but this is what she treasured most: being MOTHER to her children. And her children, having been raised up, call her blessed! (Prov. 31:28).

Rachel with her two daughters Kristi and Carita.

Happy Mother's Day, Mom!
Posted on Facebook, May 12, 2013, by Carita

Dear Mom,

I think I still find it difficult to wrap my mind around the fact that you are not here and you are not coming back. But it's been six months now. In some ways, it's hard to believe that we've survived without you that long already; and in some ways, it feels wrong that we have. There are lots of people praying for us, though, and God is with us.

Mother's Day approaching has brought on more emotion for me again. I probably appreciate the day more than I ever did before, and that makes me sad. I'm sorry, Mom, for not appreciating you like I should have when you were here. I'm sorry for, at times, scorning your ideas and dreams. Thank you for never scorning mine. Thank you for being a good Mom to me and for loving me, though I wasn't always the respectful daughter that I should've been.

I miss you, Mom. I miss the stability your presence was to our family. Something we couldn't even realize until you were gone—snatched away from us in less than an hour, crushed to the point that you couldn't have survived without a miracle. I miss your friendship to me, and the rest of our family (and to others beyond our family). I miss being able to talk to you about life and its dilemmas. I miss the perspective you contributed to our family unit.

Thank you, Mom, for helping to instill into my heart the truths that prayer works and that God is good no matter what. Thank you for helping to give me the skills I need to survive without you. Thank you most of all for, with Dad, teaching me about God.

The pain that your absence brings is overwhelming to us at times. I don't really like it; I don't like hurting. But it is a reminder that I loved you—and still do! I still don't understand why you had to go now, and need to choose to trust that, in it all, God has a good plan—though it doesn't feel very good.

I probably value Mother's Day more now because I'm not taking you for granted anymore. I wish I had a Mother here to call, to buy a card/gift for, to celebrate. And not just any Mother. I wish I had *my* Mom.

The tears have been with me this week. Not the gut-wrenching sobs of sometimes. Just gentle, but pain-filled, tears for what I have lost. You probably sometimes wondered if we really valued you— but, oh Mom! We need you. We miss you. We love you. I need you. I miss you. *I love you!*

You really were the best mom a child could have. You loved. You disciplined. You cared. You prayed. You taught. You listened. You wanted us and you wanted to be with us.

I don't know if I've accepted your death or not. But, I do know that God is with me, and He's working in me—in us ... painful though it is.

We frequently sing "We Place You on the Highest Place." Sometimes when we get to the last line—"And we come to You and worship at Your feet"—I picture you worshipping at the feet of Jesus. That's what we're doing, too, but you're just a bit closer to Him. We worship together at the feet of Jesus.

Tonight, as we sang with friends, I thought of you and your favorite song (or one of them): "There is a Redeemer." We sang the song, "What a Friend We Have in Jesus," and I remembered that when I was a child that was your favorite song. Later, on our way home, people were talking about the restaurant, Panda Express, and I remembered that you really liked that restaurant.

This year for Mother's Day, I'll take flowers to a grave. It brings tears to my eyes just thinking about it now. I'll honor you by wearing lavender. We may sing one of your favorite songs. Dad and I will visit the Forest Lawn Mural and end up in tears when the "Resurrection" scene is shown and the "Hallelujah Chorus" is played.

There are so many thoughts in my heart. I wish you were here so I could give you a hug and apologize for not respecting you more—that apology that I thought of, but never got around to giving, and then you were gone. And I wish you were here for so many more reasons. Yet, I know that you are the one in a better place—I wish that felt more real to me.

In the meantime, I cling to God ... learning to go to Him with my burdens and to trust Him. I've inherited your worries.

But I also have your God to whom you were learning to give your fears. He is my God, too, and I continue to learn to rest in Him as well.

I love you, Mom. Thanks for being my Mom!

Dear Jesus,

Thank You for giving me such a beautiful Mom. Thank You for all she taught and passed on to me. Thank You that You are with me, even though she can no longer be with me. Thank You that You love me and care about me even more than she did—which was very much. Thank You that You are seeing/carrying us along this difficult path. I love You.

Carita with her mother at her high school graduation.

By Kristi Witmer, December 22, 2014 at 8:18pm.
(Rachel's birthday was December 23.)

Mom: Few women have influenced and affected my life as she has. Who I am today, the way I think, the way I process and "do" life—are largely a result of her intentional mothering.

And all those conversations with her? Priceless—it's amazing what a brain can remember, even subconsciously, from the days-gone-by. All that input, all the prayer times together and simply hanging out, just being. I would never trade those "wasted" mornings of sitting around talking and getting nothing done, or the late nights when we wondered why we weren't just going to bed and getting some sleep already.

She showed me what it looks like to be comfortable in one's own skin—recognizing and being okay with being human and imperfect—and yet always striving to be more like Jesus, to be the best wife, mother, and friend she could be.

Hardly a day goes by that I don't think of her, but especially tonight, as I anticipate her birthday tomorrow and wonder what we'd do to celebrate if she were here.

TONIGHT :
- I celebrate the fact that God brought Rachel Hope into this world
- I celebrate having the privilege of being her daughter
- I celebrate memories
- I celebrate the hope of one day being together again, in the presence of Jesus.

Kristi with her mother at her senior year photo
shoot in Huntington Gardens.

Final Moments, Memories and Thoughts
November 26, 2012, by aguyonajourney, Marcel's blog

I write, not because I feel like I have profound things to say, but because I seek to remember a profound woman. I write also to quench my thirst for healing. I seek to put into words – into the archives of human journals – my memories and thoughts of the lady who brought me into this world and prepared me for life without her.

I remember when I was getting ready to leave this summer and was about all packed up and ready to head out with my friends Mike and Benji across the country to a new life and my new Love, Mom came into my almost-empty room. She looked at me with a nostalgic eye and gave me a hug. She then broke down in a soft, but intense, cry. I hugged her close. She apologized. I remember saying, "It's ok to cry, Mom." I was the first to leave home for good. I assumed she was full of nostalgia. And I think she probably assumed the same. Now, in light of everything, I wonder if Mom was broken up for reasons she did not even know: unknown to us, our time together on earth was nearing its final days. After that goodbye I spent only eight more days in her presence (the eight days she and the rest of my family were in Lancaster before mine and Krista's wedding).

The last day I saw my Mom was the day Krista and I were married. I barely remember her from that day. I wish I could remember more of her from that day, as I never saw her alive again after that. I don't even remember saying good-bye to her specifically that day. I know I did, because I vaguely remember the context. Krista and I had just returned to the church from a post-reception photo shoot to say good-bye to our families. We caught my Dad and Mom, Aunt Miriam, Uncle Lester, and Cousin Hannah in the parking lot of the church. We hurriedly said good-bye to them; we probably hugged them as well. But I don't remember that last hug I gave my Mom. As hard as I try, I cannot remember it. One never sees profound moments until they are past.

Marcel with his mother at his wedding.

Though I cannot remember that hug, I do have a couple special memories of my Mom from that day. I remember standing at the back of the sanctuary waiting for the song to start which would signal me to escort her to her seat at the front of the sanctuary. I remember standing there and both of us gazing over the crowd, whispering about different people who were there. I asked if my Uncle Tim and Aunt Lynette had made it. She said, "Yes, didn't you see them?" and pointed with her gaze to where they were sitting. We gazed over the crowd a bit more, then we both stood there, silently, choked with the emotion of the moment. I remember looking over and seeing tears in her eyes. The song began, and I escorted her to her seat. I gave her a tight squeeze at the end of the aisle (this is the last hug I remember giving her). Then I turned and went back down the aisle to escort Krista's mom to her seat. The other memory I have of my Mom from that day is her hand on my shoulder when our parents were praying their "prayer of blessing."

In the month between our honeymoon and when we were to leave to go to Colorado for Asher's wedding, I think I called my Mom once. I regret that. I wish I would have called her at least once more. I remember thinking that I should call her, I had talked to Dad a couple times, but it was time to talk to Mom again. But I was busy, and it kept getting pushed off.

The conversation that I did have in that month was a fun and relaxed conversation: it rambled from one subject to the next with nothing in particular needing to be discussed. We hung up from that conversation with a casual "goodnight" – the last "goodnight" I ever said to my Mom. She hung up and headed toward her bed, toward Colorado, toward the trip to Walmart, toward the intersection of Colorado 67 and Fremont County Rd. 123, toward the path of a Dodge Ram pickup truck …

★★★★★

I think one of the most difficult things about my Mom's death is that I was not there to say one last goodbye. I was not there to hang out with her one last time. I was not there to arrive at the scene of the accident. I was not there to see her broken body with my own eyes. I was not there to see her whisked off in the helicopter toward Penrose-St. Francis Hospital. I was not there when the doctors told my family she had not made it. It all feels so distant at times, so hard to believe. And it's already almost three weeks since it all happened.

I first found out about it from my sister Kristi, who sent a simple text to me while I was at work at my desk in Pennsylvania. All it said was "Pray for us. We were just hit by a car." This text clued me into events that broke my heart and have changed my life.

The image of the incredible crushing force of a 4X4 pickup truck going close to 60 mph slamming cold metal into my precious Mom and her completely feminine and gentle body simply staggers my mind. When I looked at the van and saw how the driver's side of the van was crinkled like a pop can crinkles when you take your foot and stomp on it, I felt like vomiting.

Mom? Dead? What does this mean? It's hard to wrap my mind around the finality of it all.

What about my wife? She was supposed to get to know Mom as her mother-in-law. And my kids were supposed to know her as their gentle and wise grandmother. Nothing brought Mom more joy than her family. She loved family like no one else I know. She loved her husband, her children, her son's wives, her parents, her siblings, her sibling's spouses, her nieces and nephews. Her heart had an amazing capacity to love even when pushed away, to pursue even when told to give up, to encourage even when those she loved were incorrigible. She was constantly believing and hoping in them and in her God.

She taught Truth. She constantly reminded people to know who they are in Christ, to not believe lies, but to believe God's Truth. She taught this, not as one who constantly had victory herself in these areas, but as one who struggled daily to do the same.

Grief. What does it look like? I find that even in grief I have expectations. And worship, what does that look like?

A portion of my journal says this: *The excruciating pain. And we are told to worship. To worship our Good God. I struggle with this. I have to be honest, I struggle with this. For I do not feel like worshiping. I do not feel like admitting that this is from a Good God. I want to point this out to God as an incredible accident in his plan for Creation. For this was not to happen! 'Look, see all these old women? She was supposed to live long like them and become old and senile so that we had to take care of her and meet her needs. And while she was getting old, she was supposed to mentor and love my wife and invest and care for my children as a loving Grandmother.'*

Those are my feelings. But … but … my dear sweet mother would always tell us, "Don't live life based on your feelings … Don't go by your feelings … Believe Truth.

I choose today to declare that God is Good. I cling to God not being able to see anything else. I cling to him though the mist is thick. I cling to him, though it is cold and my hands are numb and I cannot even feel my hand against his. But I know he is there. I have worshiped and clung to him throughout all the good times in life, so I will not give up when bad times exist.

The day after my Mom's memorial service in Los Angeles, my Grandpa read this verse at breakfast: Psalm 95:6-7, "O come, let us worship and bow down: let us kneel before the Lord our maker.

For he is our God; and we are the people of his pasture, and the sheep of his hand."

To kneel and bow down before the Lord, our maker – for He is an "awesome, good, and wonderful God" is my chosen response.

LET IT BE SAID OF US
by Steve Fry

"Let it be said of us that the Lord was our passion,
That with gladness we bore every cross we were given;
That we fought the good fight, and we finished the course;
Knowing within us the power of the risen Lord.
"Let the cross be our glory and the Lord be our song!
By mercy made holy, by the Spirit made strong.
Let the cross be our glory and the Lord be our song!
Till the likeness of Jesus be through us made known.
Let the cross be our glory and the Lord be our song.
Let it be said of us, we were marked by forgiveness;
We were known by our love and delighted in mercy;
We were ruled by His peace, heeding unity's call,
Joined as one body that Christ would be seen by all."

(Song sung at Krista's & my wedding – 57 days before the accident)

And in the words of the nineteenth century poet Rilke:
But because being here is much and because
all this
that's here, so fleeting, seems to require us
and strangely
concern us. Us the most fleeting of all.
Just once,
everything, only for once. Once and no more.
And we, too,
once. And never again. But this
having been once, though only once,
having been once on earth -- Can it ever be canceled?

Mom, though your body was laid in the ground and swallowed up by the earth -- I cannot and will not say goodbye. For you will forever be stamped into my "once."

… No, it can never be canceled.

I love you, Mom! Happy Mother's Day!
-Marcel

One Thing Mom Did Well We All Should Learn
May 9, 2014 / Blog post by Asher

Mothers are amazing people. They don't get near enough credit! They work so hard and do so much and barely get a "Thank you for the meal" at the end of the day. It blesses me that so many Mom's faithfully serve their families with joy, in spite of the lack of recognition they sometimes receive.

But it blows me away to meet a Mother that goes beyond the hard work and proper care and invests something even more strenuous into their families. Those women are not just *good* Mothers, they are the *saints* of all Mothers. And they have something that each of us should develop.

My Mom was one of those mothers. If you don't mind, I'm going to brag on her a bit, today. You see, this is the second Mother's Day that I have not had her alive to celebrate. My Mom was not perfect. At times I felt she was nosy. Other times, I got frustrated with her because she didn't seem to care. Perhaps I was being immature, but let's be real: no Mom is perfect. Possibly, the one's that try to *be* perfect end up missing their kids hearts the most. That wasn't my Mom. She knew she wasn't perfect …

… but that didn't keep her from excelling as a Mom.

Mom did her best to be thrifty. She kept a clean home, and she tried hard to keep me eating healthy, despite my craving for sweets. But that's not what I remember the most about Mom. What sticks in my mind of Mom, is her *value for relationships*. She held her relationship with us kids higher than whether or not she got the best deal, or whether or not we were the skinniest family. She was okay if her life wasn't all together …

… as long as she had good relationships with her kids.

Daughters need it for knowing how to invite others into relationships. Sons need it for empowerment as they move out into relationships. Mom excelled *as* a Mom because she valued relationships. She considered *relationships* as more important than a clean house, healthy diet, or thrifty shopping. Her life lives on, today, because of the relationships she nurtured.

If any of us are going to truly succeed in life, whether man or women, we need to value *relationships* above everything else in this life because that's what God designed us for.

Mom

A mom is security, love and support;
She knows what you're about, both inside and out.
You tell her the latest, the good and the bad,
And caringly she listens to the heart of the sad.

—

From childhood to grown up
She's there in the midst.
She's everything that matters
Like a precious jewel she sparkles and shimmers.

—

But you take her for granted.
Yet her love is not lessened,
Diminished or slanted—
It's within her deeply planted.

—

And then,

—

You wake up and find,
The gem afore spoken
Sits there and is broken;
She's moaning and groaning
And running out of time.

—

Oh what I would do,
Looking back with regret,
To whisper her name again and again.

To sing her sweet songs.
Oh how I do long
To shout with my life

—

I LOVE YOU, MOM!

—

I would tear down the sky
Just to say one last good-bye.
To hug her and kiss her
And let her see me cry.

—

The tears run so easy
Like never before,
She loved us so much—
Why didn't I love her more?

—

But now she is gone,
Taken beyond,
To a land without shadow
A place that is hallow.

—

She's traveled to Heaven
She's taken to Jesus
And Jesus can love her
'Cause He's the true lover.

—

And though I can't see it,
And hardly believe it:
I rest in this promise
For I know He will keep it.
C.D. (Christopher Daniel)

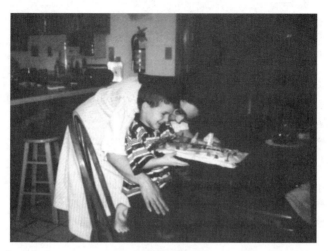

Rachel with her youngest son Christopher on his fourth birthday.

This from our dear Minnesota friends, Pastor Jack and Anna Tillotson of the Cloverdale Mennonite Church:

> *You continue to be in our prayers … Your wife and mother, Rachel, was indeed a gracious, joyful servant who connected in deep, heartfelt ways with many. She lived out her life in "fear and trembling" – profound reverence and awe toward God – pointing others to Jesus. Mother's Day this year will be oh, so different for you all. We are asking and trusting our heavenly Father in His tenderness and love to carry you and to bless you in special ways as you remember and celebrate your mother and wife for the wonderful lady she was.*
>
> *With love, Jack and Anna Tillotson*

Reflections in Marriage

5. The Intimate Relationship (Bridegroom)

THE REAL THING:

Christ is in the midst of the Church. The testimony of Christ is:

"I will declare thy name unto my brethren, in the midst of the church will I sing praise unto thee" (Heb. 2:12).

"And in the midst of the seven candlesticks one like unto the Son of man" (Rev. 1:13a).

THE REFLECTION:

The husband is emotionally connected with his wife (certainly there is a physical and sexual element as well, but wives feel this connection primarily in emotional, mental, and spiritual ways).

"So ought men to love their wives as their own bodies. He that loveth his wife loveth himself. For no man ever yet hated his own flesh; but nourisheth and cherisheth it, even as the Lord the church:" (Eph 5:28_29).

A beautiful type of Christ in the midst of the church making their relationship complete!

"How-tos" For Couples

She Honored My Passion for CONQUEST

Contentment was the state Rachel lived in, but she was married to a man who loved conquest. And while she would have been perfectly happy in a much smaller world, she came to love my long-range vision and instinctive urge to conquer the next horizon.

R = ___Relationships___: Face to face in marriage; shoulder to shoulder with my friends.

A = ___Authority___: The desire to serve and to lead is the essence of authority and manhood.

C = ___Conquest___: God has put within every male image-bearer of Himself this chromosome.

H = _____: Something within the genes of a man longs to provide for and protect those under his care.

E = _____: Many women are shame-based in their approach to men. But this is the opposite of shame.

L = _____: This is powerful to a man. An honoring woman believes in her man more than he believes in himself.

Now not every man is exactly like me in this regard, yet God has put within every male image-of-Himself the chromosome of conquest. But many women are afraid of it—this fear usually stems back to either neglect or abuse by the early father image in their lives. Of course, as men, we need to be tempered by our Creator and tuned into our counterparts, but conquer we will if we're allowed!

I believe this is where some of the sexual addictions come into play for men. When men are not honored for the romantic, visionary, "give me this mountain" kind of ambition that Caleb had in the Bible, they will shrivel into lusting, pornographic imaginaries instead. For wives, this has to do with husbands, but even more powerfully for mothers, it has to do with their impact upon sons. Let me say it another way: When sons are not honored for that certain visionary romanticism they're born with, they will shrivel into lusting, pornographic imaginaries.

Rachel with her sons Marcel, Christopher, and Asher.

If real men are assured of understanding and honored in their privacy, this will move them deeply. In fact, I'd guess most men right now have just felt their eyes moisten up a bit, because none of us are proud of our vulnerabilities in this area. In fact, we hate it! But we must embrace it! To do this, it is absolutely imperative that we not only be allowed to pursue our passions but are encouraged to do so. And those passions will be honorable for men who are honored for passion.

My boys found masculine passion modeled in me, but much of its empowerment came from their mother. As frightened as she sometimes was to cut the apron strings and let her sons go, she believed in their destinies more than her own designs for them and would have found it even more excruciating to try to corral them in. That's why she signed off on allowing Asher as a sixteen-year-old to board a plane with one of his friends and fly halfway around the world (to a place where he and his wife and two young sons now live and where he is teaching at a missionary school in Thailand). That's also why she stood in Marcel's bedroom weeping as she watched him pack his things together to move out of our home and head for Lancaster County, Pennsylvania, to marry his girlfriend and pursue a career in medicine. And again, this is why, ever since his mother's passing, Christopher has struggled like a wounded warrior to believe in himself and fight his way through to God, again and again and again, while all along taking strides toward maturity far beyond his years and making connections in ministry unimaginable to others.

And this, too, is why I've hobbled along through a foreign fog, barely making out sketches of truth and reality from the demonic shadows that seem to lurk around every corner I turn. The power of passion burning within but no passionate lover to lure it out. I fast and I hike and sometimes I hike fast … and it's good I do, because if I didn't, I'd probably soon turn into something between a couch potato and a poached egg. God said it best: "It's not good for man to be alone."

But every scenic highway is a two-way road, not a freeway. So my survival is a combination of God's good grace, His good people, and my good sense. Rachel honored my passion for conquest, because she knew my passion for her. So the Lord honors me as I honor Him. Again let me say it to all of us men: Let's pursue God like our lives depend on it (they do), and let's go after our wives so they can come after us … AND our conquests (they will)!

If I Could Send a Letter to Heaven
Posted on Facebook, May 12, 2013, by Kristi

Mom,

It is hard for me to believe that you've been in Heaven for six months now. My mind often wanders to where you are and I often wish I could join you there. I miss having you here—your smile and laughter; your insight; your love for people, especially your family. I miss the way you lived life fully—you searched God's heart for the answers to your questions about life. You were always learning and growing. I miss spending time with you—sitting in your bedroom asking you questions and talking about absolutely anything that came to our minds. I miss your input into my life. I miss talking to you on the phone when we are apart. Have we really been apart for six months and not talked on the phone at all? And yet I still find myself tucking things away in my memory to tell you the next time I get a chance to talk to you or e-mail you.

It's Mother's Day. Your day. The day set aside for celebrating you because you are my Mom. Yet, this year the celebration is touched with pain because you are not here with us for the celebration. I can only imagine the joy and wonder you must be experiencing—really the best gift you could have on Mother's day. Yet, for us left behind, this day serves as a reminder of your absence and of how much I miss you.

My heart aches for another chance to be together with you—to celebrate you with you—and to thank you for all you were to me and taught me in the years that we did have together. Yet while my heart aches for your presence, I can't help but continue to celebrate who you were, the relationship we had together, and all that we experienced together. I can celebrate the life you have given me and lived before me.

Thank you, Mom, for living those 19 years so faithfully with me. For making right choices, for setting an example and leaving a legacy of following God that I can now look back on and continue to learn from even though you are not with me anymore. I think of my relationship with God and how much you affected it and poured into it, pointing me toward Him over and over again as I grew and faced new stages of life. Thank you for encouraging me to seek Christ with all my heart and to follow wherever He leads, even when it's hard and scary. Thanks for teaching me that by living it.

You prayed, Mom. I remember various times when you would remind me to talk to Jesus about life and the things that are on my heart—whether dreams and aspirations or fears and struggles—because He is the best one to talk to about those things. And you exemplified a life of prayer, praying for us children as we grew up and headed out into life, praying for Dad as he led the family into unknown places, praying for other friends and loved ones. I remember not so long ago, when you read the verse in Revelation that talks of the prayers of the saints mixing with incense and ascending to God and how much it meant to you on behalf of friends you loved so much who no longer had their mother here on earth. It meant so much to you, because it gave you a word picture of how God is still receiving and hearing the prayers of parents who have already passed on. Little did you know how much your own children would need to know that. I have clung to that verse so much since then.

You involved yourself in the lives of others and cared passionately for what they were facing. You cared because you wanted to see them experience God and know His love. You were always so interested in the lives of others—asking questions, listening, showing value to people that crossed your path.

Thank you for sharing your journey with me—for not only letting me in on your victories and strengths but also on your struggles and weaknesses. I think of your openness in dealing with fear and your readiness to combat fear with faith in God. Rather than living life in the shadows of what could happen, you stepped forward in the light of God's truth and stood firm on His promises even when it was difficult. And you were always ready to learn and tell about what you had learned in your journey, giving glory to God for His work in your life. Thank you for teaching me what it means to be a learner, to continually be searching God's heart and learning more and more about what it means to follow and imitate Him.

I could go on much longer about what you have gave me in the 19 years of our lives together, but this year the thing that I'm realizing more than ever is just how much you invested in my life and prepared me for this time in my life—The words of life and truth that you spoke into my life that I can now look back on and remember and cling to as I continue to grow and face this life on earth. The relationship with Jesus you exemplified and encouraged me to live. Jesus—the only strength to cling to and constant to depend on when all else is falling apart. Thank you Mom for seeking His heart passionately and for leading the way and setting an example that I can continue to follow even though I cannot be with you anymore.

I love you so much, Mom, and miss you like crazy. I wish we could be together today, but I am so grateful for the years of life we had together and for all that I can take with me from here because of your influence on my life.

All of the children around their mother's grave.

A status update from my Mom on October 14, 2012, less than a month before her death.

Rachel Witmer

"*We never need to be without hope. For as we look into the future with the eyes of faith,*
We will see God is already there." –Roy Lessin

CHAPTER 13

Her Labors of Love

Rachel's Story

"Well reported of for good works; if she have brought up children, if she have lodged strangers, if she have washed the saints' feet, if she have relieved the afflicted, if she have diligently followed every good work" (1 Tim. 5:10).

Dictionaries define "labor of love" as work done for interest in the work itself or for the benefit of others, rather than for payment. The focus is on others and on the work being done for others. It's the opposite of self-focus. Whether it's raising your kids, feeding the homeless, or shepherding the church, if there's even a smidgen of self-focus involved, it's a doubtful labor of love.

We can understand this in terms of monetary benefit or reward, but what about other less obvious methods of payment? What about verbal accolades or even quiet compliments from others? What about that subtle self-image we carefully manage and protect? If there's something in it for me, it can hardly be considered a labor of love, other than self-love perhaps.

By contrast, humility is not necessarily thinking less of one's self. Rather, it's simply not thinking of one's self at all. But for some people, life's all about self. Everything … it's always all about them! What should Christians like this be called anyway? Aberrations: the act of departing from the right, normal, or usual course; lapsing from a sound mental state (Dictionary.com). Jude, the servant of Jesus, calls them "wandering stars" (Jude 13). They have their own little world and are smack in the middle of it. They have good relationships with others as long as those relationships serve their interests or make them look good. They're all excited about ministry as long as it puts a halo over their heads or somehow adds to their resume. It's the opposite of humility; it's a SELF-focus. It's certainly laborious, but it's not a labor of love.

Rachel was authentically inclined toward others. She was obsessed with her Schrader siblings. She pursued them even when some didn't always reciprocate. And she'd use whatever means she had at her disposal to connect with them. Often she'd sit up late here in California thumbing out texts to them two or three time zones away. She was also intentional about her parents. She sometimes talked about how they should come live with us when they became elderly. Recently her parents were saying that they had always kinda planned to see if they could move in with her and her family when they couldn't take care of themselves anymore. It breaks my heart to think of it, because I know she'd have been delighted with that. I increasingly see her death as a direct attack from Satan in so many ways. But God is greater, and everyone who aligns with Him will win!

Even more than she was tuned into her siblings and parents, Rachel was intently tuned into her children. There was no part of their lives she would have been remise to be interested in. Apron strings were tough for her to sever. As a model mom, nothing could have defined her labors of love better.

And as a pastor's wife, even though there were emotionally exhausting demands to the role, she tirelessly pursued connection with the ladies in our fellowship circles. She didn't consider herself to be a leader, nor was she naturally disposed toward organizational things, but she'd organize an event if she had to—even lead if she must, and she certainly was always ready be part of team efforts to reach out to others to serve, counsel, and comfort.

Teenagers, ill at rest in their own homes, found repose in the environment Rachel created. While she engaged them in conversations they should have been having with their own parents, she had a thoughtful way of turning their hearts homeward. She also cared for the elderly in ways that brought dignity back into their lives, welcoming them into her home with enough love to reach all the way around.

Particularly in the last years of her life here in Los Angeles, she even found room for the homeless—those who had nothing to offer in return, except their gratitude. And while I was usually their point of contact, when she was suddenly snatched from us, they were completely devastated and felt homeless again, like she had been their last straw for survival.

These were her labors of love. This was how Rachel lived life and loved it. There is a hallowed sanctuary in the hearts of everyone whose lives she has graced in one way or another at some time or other. She was not about herself! She had a focus beyond what average folks can even see. And today she has a vision and perspective from heaven's heights that all whom she loved can feel despite her absence. This lies large in her legacy— her labor of love for so many.

The Bride of Christ

How did Rachel's life in this regard portend the Bride of Christ? The church is a Bride, a body, a family, an ark of safety, and so much more. The church is engaged to Him and eagerly awaits her full consummation upon His return. She loves Him, can't stop thinking about Him, and hangs onto every word He's said. She embraces His purposes and makes His vision her own. She knows that in giving herself to Him, she has His all too.

So much of Rachel's labors of love were dilations of my own passions. She took them, made them her own, enlarged upon them, and incarnated them in ways I could never do. So the church does with the passions of Christ's heart. She so beautifully fulfills His purposes and impassions His vision for the world. She is His body: He has no hands but her hands, no feet but her feet, and might I add, no heart but her heart. The body of Christ completes His purposes in the world.

Teaching lessons from Rachel's life at Evening Bible Camp, 2013.

And she does this all in the context of family. She's a community. While there is a bridal intimacy with Christ, there is also the communal association of family. She reaches out to others and wraps her arms around them in ways no one else but the family of God can do. It's not *just* warm and fuzzy, but it *is* warm and fuzzy. It's not *just* about the accountability that comes with a common surname, but it *is* about accountability—accountability to the Name of Christ. We are **Christ**ians after all. Christ claims us for His own! He says, "MY church," and He also says, "this is MY body … broken for you" (Matt. 16:18; Luke 22:19). The church is all about love and relationships, but it's also all about identity, belonging, and having all things in common with each other (Acts 2:44).

The church of Christ—bride, body, and family—is also that ark of safety to all those bobbing around on the ocean of life. With all of life's high rollers and rip currents, sharks and sting rays, pelting rain and blasting sun—yes, all of us need that ark of safety where we are sheltered and given navigational direction. If this is what we are receiving, we can know it's the true church. If a turmoil within matches the tumult without, then what we're in is not the real thing. We shouldn't just *be* safe, we should also *feel* safe. (But just because we don't *feel* safe, doesn't always mean we *aren't* safe; not feeling safe can be an unresolved issue from our past.) True security comes from Jesus and our identity with Him. That's what makes the church a real ark of safety!

The sad truth is that, in terms of emotional and relational maturity, too little difference exists between Christians inside the church and those outside who make no claim of having a relationship with Jesus Christ. More alarmingly, when you go beyond the Sunday morning worship service into the homes and small groups of God's people, you often find a valley littered with broken and failed relationships. In fact, for many the entry point into the next personal or social relationship is a straight shot from a previous relationship failure. Church hopping is more about unresolved-broken-relationship-hopping than anything else.

Such church hoppers may present themselves as spiritually mature, but something is terribly imbalanced about their spirituality. Many are "spiritually mature" but remain infants, children, or teenagers emotionally. They demonstrate little ability to process anger, sadness, or hurt. They whine, complain, distance themselves, blame, and use sarcasm—like children when they don't get their way. Highly defensive to criticism or differences of opinion, they expect to be taken care of and often use people to meet their own needs.

The roots of this problem lie in a faulty spirituality, stemming from a faulty biblical theology. Many Christians have received helpful instruction in certain essential areas of discipleship, such as prayer, Bible study, worship, discovery of their spiritual gifts, or learning how to explain the gospel to someone else. Yet Jesus' followers also need training and skills in how to look beneath the surface of the iceberg of who they are, to break the power of how their past influences the present, to live in brokenness and vulnerability, to know their limits, to embrace their loss and grief, to make incarnation their model for loving well, and to slow down in order to live with integrity. Loving God and others well simultaneously is emotionally healthy spirituality. They are mutually inclusive; without both, neither one can exist.

Despite all the emphasis today on spiritual formation, churches rarely address what real spiritual maturity looks like as it relates to emotional health. For this reason, our churches are filled with people who remain emotionally unaware and socially immature. It's sad, but I can think of a number of unbelievers who are more loving, balanced, and civil than many church members I know (including myself). The link between emotional health and spiritual maturity is a large, unexplored area of discipleship. We desperately need, I believe, to reexamine the whole of Scripture—and the life of Jesus in particular—in order to grasp the dynamics of this link.

"The Bride is beautiful ... but she is married to another man."

This phrase of uncertain origin has been cited by scholars and in publications as the text of a cable sent by a Jewish fact-finding mission to Palestine in the 1890s.[2] It is generally portrayed as an early but ignored implication that a Jewish homeland could not be reestablished in Palestine without interfering with the existing population.[3] Historian Anthony Pagden quotes the phrase in his book *Worlds at War: The 2,500-Year Struggle Between East and West*, explaining that its implication was "that the Zionists should attempt to marry someone else."[4]

---

[2]   Shai Afsai, "The 'Married to another Man' Story," *Jewish Ideas Daily*, October 12, 2012.

[3]   Benjamin Beit-Hallahmi, *Original Sins: Reflections on the History of Zionism and Israel* (Palgrave Macmillan, 1992), p. 74.

[4]   Eric Silver, "Decade of Disillusion," *The Guardian*, June 4, 1977, p.7; Anthony Pagden, *Worlds at War* (Oxford University Press, 2008), p. 419.

Sad as it sounds, this phrase often aptly describes the Bride of Christ too. When people come to faith in Christ, they become beautiful. But then they become distracted with something else. Many times those other distractions are good things but just not what we should be "married" to. And so Jesus gets ignored while we hustle after the most charismatic speaker in Christian circles or the most recent bestselling Christian book to hit the marketplace or the most novel evangelistic technique introduced since the *Romans Road* gospel tract.

Again, the Apostle Paul saw it coming when he writes to the Corinthian Christians in 2 Corinthians 11:3-4: "The thing that has me so upset is that I care about you so much—this is the passion of God burning inside me! I promised your hand in marriage to Christ, presented you as a pure virgin to her husband. And now I'm afraid that exactly as the Serpent seduced Eve with his smooth patter, you are being lured away from the simple purity of your love for Christ. It seems that if someone shows up preaching quite another Jesus than we preached—different spirit, different message—you put up with him quite nicely" (The Message).

Paul is saying essentially, I thought I'd officiated in an actual marriage of you to Christ. It was awesome to see your love and adoration for Him. You were His beautiful bride! But now it seems you're married to another man. What happened? Was Christ not good enough? Did I somehow mess up the ceremony? Or has an imposing adulterer stolen your hearts?

Reflections in Marriage

5. The Intimate Relationship (Bride)

THE REAL THING:
    The church rejoices for the fact of Christ's presence within her.
    "To whom God would make known what is the riches of the glory of this mystery among the Gentiles; which is <u>Christ in you</u>, the hope of glory" (Col. 1:27).

THE REFLECTION:
    The wife in union with her husband (for us as husbands, we feel this to a much greater extent in a physical and sexual way than for our wives). And this is not wrong, just different.

> "For this cause shall a man leave his father and mother, and shall be joined unto his wife, and they two shall be one flesh" (Eph. 5:31).
>
> Such is the most intimate relationship that can ever be experienced. It is a beautiful reflection of "Christ in you" fulfilling our God-given function.

"How-tos" For Couples

Rachel Honored Hierarchy

"Please help me," she quietly begged. But I couldn't.

Then she died, and along with her, something in me died too.

R = ___Relationships___: Face to face in marriage; shoulder to shoulder with my friends.

A = ___Authority___: The desire to serve and to lead is the essence of authority and manhood.

C = ___Conquest___: God has put within every male image-bearer of Himself this chromosome.

H = ___Hierarchy___: Something within the genes of a man longs to provide for and protect those under his care.

E = _____: Many women are shame-based in their approach to men. But this is the opposite of shame.

L = _____: This is powerful to a man. An honoring woman believes in her man more than he believes in himself.

Rachel not only understood my propensity to provide for her and protect her, but like most wives today, she counted on it! That's why billions of dollars are spent every year on life insurance policies, and most of these policies are purchased by men not wanting their wives and children to be left without provision. Yet some in our culture still get all tied up in knots about this. To them, equality means sameness. But while sameness may sound nice to some couples, it essentially renders them mutually unnecessary. No wonder our society seems sometimes like a dog chasing its tail, as in the case of our little Sheltie in the backyard with a helicopter circling overhead (as happens many times here in Los Angeles). He knows that amazing machine is up there doing something significant, but he's not sure what or how to intercept it, and so he runs around in circles barking as loud as he can, looking silly.

Arguing against Scripture is just as silly and never gets us anywhere, because God is the Author and He knows everything. But in order to benefit from its insight, we must accept its authority. Ephesians 5 puts forth the model: As men, we are pictures of Christ in His sacrifice for us on the cross to protect us from Satan and to provide for our salvation. Women picture the church in responsiveness to Christ's unconditional love for them. Their reverence for Him is rooted in His sacrifice for them. Marriage then is the honorable privilege to model such love and respect together.

Scripture goes on to say in 1 Corinthians 7:28, "If you marry ... you will have trouble." That's pretty straightforward! Unlike Hollywood, the Bible is very realistic. Marriage is difficult in large part because men and women are so different. In today's cultural atmosphere, women are often offended by the very idea of needing a man to protect them or to provide for them in some way. But as a beautiful model of the church, Rachel keenly felt her dependence upon me as her husband. In fact, the most difficult period of our marriage was when I leaned too much on her for help, and she felt the need to protect me. Though she did so valiantly, it made her feel vulnerable and unprotected herself.

But those who understand hierarchy, get it. They just do. They appreciate the hierarchical nature of men; how men are driven to serve— even die if needs be. There's something in our genes that longs to protect and provide for those in our care. And when that's missing, it's because it's been taken from us by someone ... somehow ... somewhere ... sometime.

The most gut-wrenching part of my wife's death was that I needed to watch her die, bound to a stretcher, and there was absolutely nothing I could do. I still sometimes wail in the privacy of my own experience, stumbling from chuckhole to chuckhole along the sidewalks of Los Angeles, wishing I could somehow turn things around and die for her instead of seeing her die. And every husband would feel the same way! It's inherent within us. Rachel honored that drive within me to her very last breath when she begged, "Please help me!" She was expecting me to step up to provide for her ... to protect her ... to deliver her in that most crucial hour. And when I couldn't, our marriage died.

CHAPTER 14

Brides and Apron Strings

Rachel's Story

I have so much to be thankful for! When committed couples vow "to love and to cherish, in sickness and in health, for better or for worse … till death do us part," they look forward to a full life together: honeymoon days, first home, first pregnancy, toddlers, preschoolers, adolescents, teenagers, busy years of ministry together, middle-aged years of high-school and college graduations, the empty-nest syndrome, and finally growing old together. All of this Rachel and I experienced together, save the last, unless you count turning fifty as growing old, in which case then we had it all.

So many other grieving spouses have experienced much less than I, and God always has His reasons, but He never tells us exactly why. He simply allows us to wonder and imagine as best we can, to wander along despite the confusion we feel, and to worship at both the altar of praise and the altar of lament. I wish I could wrap it all up in some sensible explanation, but I can't. All I can offer is the solution of surrender. And it really is the only solution! It's like letting a beautiful bird loose from the palm of your hand. We can grumble and grasp, but all it will do is destroy the bird or crumple its beauty. The best thing is just to release it back to God who gave it.

We can gather up all of the memorabilia and tuck it safely away in our museum of memories and visit there as often as we need to. But real resolution and healing comes in accepting the next thing God gives us: another day, another year of newfound potential, another friend, another heartfelt connection, another avenue of opportunity for growth in Christ, whom we shall meet face-to-face in the not-too-distant future, which is really what life is about anyways.

Yes, Rachel was in the midst of an intense struggle to sever her apron strings to the children. That day Marcel packed up his room was tough for her. He loaded everything into his car and headed east to Pennsylvania for final preparations with his bride Krista for their wedding day. She hugged him hard and sobbed and sobbed. The memory obviously holds deep nostalgia for him now as he recalls it time and again. It's painful, but it's precious too. That's the way this thing called grieving goes, just like cutting apron strings, both the pain and the precious happening at the same time, offering both memories to cherish and lamentable longings leading to worship. "Should we accept only good things from the hand of God and never anything bad?" (Job 2:10).

Christopher with his mother.

Her Inspiration

"Will I Ever See You Again?"
December 7, 2012 by aguyonajourney, Marcel's blog
One month … Time moves forward, memories become more distant …

It was evening. We were sitting in the living room, aching to help her. She was slipping away and there wasn't anything we could do. It was a strange living room, one I didn't recognize. We knew she was dying, but there was **nothing** we could do. She wouldn't speak; she only sat silently. There was a sense of a nearing finality, a dark feeling of time running out. Dad got up and went out the door. A while later Mom also went out the door. It was snowing outside; I remember the ground being covered in soft **white** snow. All of the sudden, I knew this was it. She was leaving. Gone. Forever.

Panicking and not knowing what to do to stop this horrible departure, I rushed to the doorway, flinging the door open. I yelled out in a broken cry with tears streaming down my cheeks, "Will I ever see you again?" She turned, standing still in the soft, **white** snow, looked at me, and with tears of pain streaming down her cheeks nodded a confident **yes**, but said nothing. Her tears of pain were from the pain of separation. She didn't say how long it would be till I saw her, but the sense was it could be a very long time, but I **would** see her again.

That was a dream I had last night. One of many I've had recently where the emotions have felt so real and the sadness heavy. But this dream, especially, brought a strange sense of comfort along with the sadness of separation that it evoked.

I know that God is good and that Heaven is real, but my faith seems so weak at times, so shaky. And I struggle with doubts. And I struggle with the tension of longing for heaven to see Mom and longing for heaven to see Christ. But, in a special way, this dream felt like a gift from God, saying, "Yes, I am here, heaven is real, you will see your Mom again someday, and it's ok to long for her!"

Worship is a choice. God is good. Belief is a choice. Heaven is real … then comes *stronger* faith. Please pray for me.

★★★★★

Rachel worried some about losing me. This is the only thing I like about her going first—she never had to experience this painful thing of losing your lover! She also dreaded the day she had to cut earth-strings with her parents; this, too, she was spared. Her parents told some in the family over our New Year's get-together that they had been hoping they could one day move in with Rachel and her family, because they felt she was the best one to take care of them when they were not able to care for themselves anymore. This touches me deeply, because I know she would have counted it the privilege of her life to do that! But it was not to be. Instead, it was divinely arranged by God the Father that they outlive their firstborn daughter and be a part of supporting her family through her death and in her absence.

As Rachel's mother sat in a chair not far from her casket suspended over the open grave on the day of her burial here at the Woodlawn Memorial Park in Glendale, she was mourning the wrenching reality of needing to watch her own daughter be buried. Her eyes were fixed on the beautiful cherry-colored casket when all of a sudden she heard Rachel's voice say, "Mom, I'm up here!" Mom looked up into the sky, and there she saw Rachel's beaming face amidst the ethereal vapors of that solemn afternoon. Heaven met earth in so many ways during those early days of separation.

The Bride of Christ

The Bride of Christ and her apron strings can be seen in how difficult it often is for founding churches to turn over the reins of leadership to the local body and its elders. Human beings were endowed in creation with instincts for survival and self-preservation. We naturally go to great lengths to help things continue as they were from the beginning. It's hard for us to imagine how something that has worked so well for so long could ever be improved by change at all, much less a change in leadership.

But life and growth is all about change. As someone recently put it, "The Spirit without the Word will cause us to blow up. And the Word without the Spirit will cause us to dry up. But the Spirit and the Word will cause us to grow up." This is what we need: to grow up! If infants never changed, we'd become alarmed and call the doctor. But by growing, these same infants move healthily through each stage of development to become strong and mature and able to partner with others in reproducing, replenishing, and bringing revival to the world around them.

The Sutera Twins of Rival Fellowship in Regina, Saskatchewan, say it succinctly, "Evangelism without revival is like holding a newborn baby up to the breast of a dead corpse." Indeed, babies born into a church fellowship where constant revival does not occur will die for lack of life and nourishment. And it doesn't matter if those babies are born from existing church families, or if they're born as a result of reaching out in evangelism. Without revival, they will die. A corpse does not emanate life. A living, moving, growing body does.

Reflections in Marriage

6. The Propagation Pattern (Bridegroom)

THE REAL THING:

Christ begets spiritual life.

"For God so loved the world that he gave his only begotten Son, that whosoever believeth in Him should not perish, but have everlasting life" (John 3:16).

THE REFLECTION:

The husband begets natural life. (Ever notice the long lists of "begets" in the Scriptures?)

"Abraham begat Isaac; and Isaac begat Jacob; and Jacob begat Judas and his brethren ..." (Mt. 1:2-16).

Propagation should not be a selfish experience, but rather one that brings joy and fulfillment to the wife. Again, a reflection of the effect that Christ has within the church.

whosoever believeth in Him should not perish, but have everlasting life" (John 3:16).

"How-tos" For Couples

Esteem: The Essence of Honor

Esteem is the opposite of shame. Most people think in terms of *self-esteem*, but Rachel had a way of giving esteem to *others*, born from a sense of knowing who she was herself. A man from our fellowship who's been next to homeless much of his life always found his sense of dignity whenever he was around her. He treated her like a queen, because she made him feel valued. I've often said Rachel was the making of me too. Her esteem for me was authentic, not the cheap stuff that feels like manipulation, but the kind that draws honor from within you like a enriching balm.

R = ___Relationships___: Face to face in marriage; shoulder to shoulder with my friends.
A = ___Authority___: The desire to serve and to lead is the essence of authority and manhood.
C = ___Conquest___: God has put within every male image-bearer of Himself this chromosome.
H = ___Hierarchy___: Something within the genes of a man longs to provide for and protect those under his care.
E = ___Esteem___: Many women are shame-based in their approach to men. But this is the opposite of shame.
L = _____: This is powerful to a man. An honoring woman believes in her man more than he believes in himself.

Many women are shame-based in their approach to men. One in three have experienced some form of sexual abuse in their lifetime, and it's universal—even Christian women within church systems, and yes, some of our Mennonite church systems too. Traumatic childhoods of abuse or neglect, turbulent teen environments, and schismatic church cultures cause them to develop warped views of men. The most traumatized are those who come from the homes of church elders and pastors where infidelity and betrayal occur. For others, they merely come from homes of permissive parenting that has them spoiled and set up for issues mirroring such complexes. These wounded women end up being severely sensitive to any inadequacies they find in men. If a man offends them or surprises them in some way, they panic and respond with daggers of ignorance, having little understanding for the masculine soul. And it's no wonder, given what they've been through!

Without healing, such women obviously do not make good wives, yet many of them run headlong into marriage. Sadly, their compulsions for marrying come from misshapen souls rather than from heartfelt fondness for their fathers modeled by their mothers. Mothers are really the only ones who can best model for their daughters a healthy affection for husbands. Without it, the need for their created counterparts is obvious but has no basis of trust to build from. Thus their relationships with men become a poisoned push/pull pattern of unresolved pain: Come here, come here, come here! Get away, get away, get away!

Praise God, though, because just as He can use good women to bring healing to men, so He can use good men to bring healing to women. It's a challenge, though, because as water finds its own level, so people of the same level of emotional health are attracted to each other. Hence, an unhealthy woman will not normally be attracted to a healthy man or vice versa. So the odds are great that her husband will be someone spiritually and emotionally healthy enough to be an aqueduct of healing to her without hurting her further. Yet all things are possible with God from whom all blessings flow. If they're both committed to health, they can inch forward step by step, year after year, grace upon grace ... bringing healing to each other.

I know these things in part, because to some degree Rachel and I lived them. We both entered marriage, nearly thirty years ago now, with an element of esteem deficiency. We were at similar levels of emotional health, but after our marriage, we faced spiritual abuse from within unhealthy church systems. This, of course, took a toll. Yet by God's amazing grace and the touch of some key friendships along the way, we were able to upper our level of emotional health, thus making it possible to elicit that element of mutual esteem so necessary for a thriving marriage. While we wounded each other some in the process of metamorphoses, by God's great mercy, and because of our determination to go for health, our wounds were limited. On balance we experienced far more healing than hurt and have been able to help others to experience the same.

So can you!

CHAPTER 15

Painful Parting!

Rachel's Story

"I am overwhelmed with joy in the Lord my God! For He has dressed me with the clothing of salvation and draped me in a robe of righteousness. I am like a bridegroom in his wedding suit or a bride with her jewels" (Is. 61:10). "Happy is that people, whose God is the Lord (Ps. 144:15b)." These verses were the last thing Rachel posted on her Facebook page, just six days before her home-going.

The text was simple that portentous Tuesday morning: "Please pray for us, we've been in an accident." It came from my daughter Kristi as I was entering the Wal-Mart there in Canon City, Colorado, where I would wait for Rachel to arrive. We had planned to help Asher and Teresa and her family prepare for their wedding, which would be held in just four days. But, out of nowhere, a hulking Dodge Ram pickup would come crashing through the driver's door, right into the delicate body of my wife. Even with side airbags, the much less sturdy Kia Sedona minivan would be no match for the hard steel framework of a four-wheel drive truck.

It was 10:40 a.m., the morning of November 6, 2012. Nothing could have prepared me for what lay ahead. Rachel and I had seldom talked about what it would be like to lose each other. We had filed an official will with the Griffith Law Office in International Falls, Minnesota, many years before and had both outlined basic funeral plans as well. She had updated hers just the year before and occasionally reminded me to update mine too. But to actually try to imagine what such a scenario would be like … it just wasn't something we wanted to do.

The text seemed fairly typical to me when I first read it: " …We've been in an accident." Different ones in our family had been in accidents over the years, and I figured it was just another fender-bender of some kind or other. But then I looked at the text again: "Please pray for us" it included. I knew Kristi was the kind of person who was quick to pray about everything, but something seemed different about this. I shook it off. *We're here in a quiet, small-town Colorado community; we're NOT in Los Angeles. This couldn't be anything too serious. Besides, we're staying with the Helmuth family, six miles out in the country.*

We had read the statistics before our move to Los Angeles, that while cities have more accidents, most fatalities happen in the country. Little could we have imagined then—moving into the second largest metropolis in the country—that one of us would come to represent that statistic precisely. And certainly not Rachel. She was the most cautious driver in the family. Maybe me or one of the boys, but certainly not her, living in the city but killed in a traffic accident out in the country.

Then my cell phone rang, overcoming the text I was staring at. It was Asher.

"Hey Dad, did you get the text from Kristi?"

"Yes, I did."

"Are you still at the Wal-Mart?"

"Yes."

"Come back out to the parking lot. Teresa and I will swing in to pick you up."

"Ok."

In a blur, I ran back out to the parking lot just in time for Asher and Teresa to come rolling up in Asher's Saturn. I jumped in the back seat as he was dialing Kristi's number to find out just where they were.

"What's the intersection where you are?" he asked her. She gave him the coordinates—an intersection hardly a mile from the Helmuths.

Upon reflection, it's pretty amazing that Kristi was able to do all of this—send out texts to the family, provide some detail about the accident, and give the exact location where the accident occurred. She, too, was in the accident, experiencing the shock of surviving an impact of this magnitude. She had also sustained a concussion and would retain hardly a memory of the day. I weep every time I think of what happened as Kristi later lay in a hospital bed. Her sister Carita had just told her about her mother's death, and she broke out into singing "Agnus Dei"—"You are Ho-ly! Ho-ly … are You Lord God Al-migh-ty! Worthy is the Lamb, worthy is the Lamb! Amen!"

It set a perfect stage for the wonderful weeping worship that was to occur over the next four days as we made both funeral plans and wedding plans simultaneously—the funeral on Friday and the wedding on Saturday. It sounds impossible, I know, but there is no worship so deeply stirring, yet supernaturally elating, as that which comes from a broken heart. Our whole family felt it that week. We've mourned many times since, bent over the altar of lament, but on the day of her funeral, our arms were lifted in rapturous wonder and worship toward a God who obviously had us in His grip.

Rachel's coffin over the grave on Resurrection
Slope at Forestlawn Memorial Park.

Rachel herself had also helped set the stage for worship at her funeral two days before her death. At Skyline Mennonite Church on Sunday where we worshipped, the service was concluded by playing a video of Ivan Parker's song, "When I Get Carried Away." It's a pretty contemporary song with heavier rhythm than Rachel would have ordinarily preferred, but I can still feel her standing beside me swaying with the powerful lyrics and music that morning, getting all "carried away" with the moment. And so it was an easy decision of mine to have that same song played at the conclusion of her funeral service, just two days later. So soon she'd been literally "carried away!"

Her Inspiration

Dancing with Jesus

My sister-in-law, Lynette Schrader, had another dream of Rachel the other night and emailed me about it. With her permission, I copy it here in her own words:

It was a sad dream for me. We were at a folk dance (I know, very unlikely). Rachel was with you and wearing a light blue dress, which looked so pretty on her. She was smiling and peaceful. Then she was gone. And you no longer had a partner for the dance. Tim and I were dancing together, and we quickly sent Ana and Alayna over to take your hands and finish the dance with you. It might sound like a silly dream, but it was so real.

I woke with tears streaming. I am teary as I write this. The reality of her passing hit me again. My tears were because I miss her. They were also for you. I felt such a crushing weight of sadness for you and your daily reality of "dancing" alone. I remind myself: ultimately we never dance alone. My prayer for you is that you feel the Father's hands holding yours as you make your way through today's dance.

This describes it so aptly! It *is* a "daily reality" to be "dancing" alone. The weight of sadness many times feels crushing. At the same time, I truly do "feel the Father's hands holding mine as I make my way through today's dance." I call it "Dancing with Jesus." With Him, I'm doing my best. We have many exhilarating times even though I stumble some with my steps. It's also wonderful to know that with HIM as my dancing partner, I'm always on His mind, and I'm forever in His heart! Won't you let Him be your dancing partner too?

★★★★★

Asher drove right to the intersection, but it was so crowded with emergency vehicles, neighbors' cars, and passersby that he couldn't park. I bailed out of the car and sprinted the 300 yards out into the desert where the minivan had come to a stop. The entire driver's side was smashed in from where the four-wheel drive pickup truck had hit it. As I approached the vehicle, an officer stopped me and told me I couldn't go closer. I told him my wife was in it.

Stay back," he repeated.

But I didn't. I moved around to the passenger side, opposite from where the ambulance crew was ripping the driver's door off with the Jaws of Life. I crawled into the passenger seat on my hands and knees and began to talk to Rachel. She was gently moaning.

"I'm here, Honeybunch! Everything's going to be alright. I love you, Rachel!"

"Please, Jesus! Have mercy ... deliver her now! Lord, nothing is impossible with You! Please, please we need You so much!"

With a screeching crunch, the driver's door came off and the rescue team carefully extricated Rachel from the van, laying her out on a stretcher. I knelt beside her as the EMTs worked to stabilize her condition. When they placed an oxygen mask over her face, she immediately tried to take it off, quietly saying to me, "Please, help me."

"That's a good sign," said one of the medics. "It's the first she's spoken. She must have recognized your voice."

"Yes, I believe she did," I said.

"I'm here with you, Rachel! We're going to get through this."

"Oh, God, please help her to breathe," I begged.

I didn't realize the massive extent of Rachel's internal injuries. Her entire rib cage was shattered, and several of the razor-sharp, jagged ends of her ribs had slit open her pericardium, the double-walled sac around her heart. Her heart was completely outside the sac. Her aorta was ruptured. She had hemorrhaging to the brain. Any one of these things would have killed her, but the coroner listed "blunt trauma to the heart" as the cause of her death. Apart from a miracle, there was no way Rachel could have survived. But, of course, I didn't know any of this at the time. I only knew she had spoken and the medic had said it was a good sign. As they slipped her stretcher into the Life Flight helicopter, I kissed Rachel on the cheek and said, "I'll see you soon."

But immediately after liftoff, as the helicopter headed for Colorado Springs, Rachel's heart stopped and the medics could never get it started again. The nurse on board later told me he'd never seen anything like it. In all his years of experience, he had never seen anyone die on board a Life Flight. Ordinarily, if the victims are so severely injured, they never make it that far, and if they make it onto a Life Flight, they normally survive. He said the fact that Rachel had lived so long with such incredible injuries is a miracle in itself. "I'll never forget that Life Flight experience," he said, "and the grace with which she gazed around the helicopter cabin, then simply closed her eyes and died."

Both Kristi and Christopher were taken by ambulance to a local hospital, and both were released within a couple of hours. Both had minor concussions, although Kristi had significant short-term memory loss and remembers very little about that day. She'd ask the same questions over and over again to those surrounding her, but she never asked a second time about her mother's death. Such sudden and significant loss could simply not be forgotten.

Teresa's father, Brother Loren Miller, drove me to the hospital in Colorado Springs where Rachel was taken. It took about an hour to get there, but it seemed an eternity. Asher, Teresa, and her brother Austin went with us. Hospital staff showed us to a little waiting room when we got there, and we waited and waited and waited. Finally, the chaplain and a doctor came. Their words were simple and to the point, referring to the team of medics who were on board the Life Flight: "They did all they could, but couldn't get her heart started again."

How does one absorb such awful words? How do twenty-eight years of marriage and myriads of "for better or for worse" end so suddenly? It really doesn't. Just yesterday, over two years later, as we sang "Agnus Dei" again in church, I shook with sobs, reliving the emotion of it all. Grace, is all I know. What I remember so distinctly is simply accepting it at the time. Grief and tears and agonizing loneliness would come later, but in the urgency of the moment when I needed it most, God's grace was there! Long-term, sustaining grace would come in time as well.

The Bride of Christ

First Critical Concern for the Church: <u>SEQUENCE</u>

Sequence is all about putting first things first. In the book of Genesis, we find a motif that is supported throughout the rest of Scripture. It has to do with the Tree of Life versus the Tree of the Knowledge of Good and Evil. The context is God and His first followers, two people whom He had just made, on a cool walk through a garden. You could say it was the first place God ever met with His people; the first church, if you please. It wasn't a house church (there was no house) but a home fellowship. And their home was a garden ... the Garden of Eden. This is where God met with them.

The Tree of Life, along with all the other trees in the garden, was wide open for this couple to eat from. But one tree in the middle of the garden God specifically commanded them not to eat from: the Tree of the Knowledge of Good and Evil. Why? Why did God go to the bother of making such a tree, bearing obviously delicious fruit, but then tell them not to eat from it? God's answer was direct and to the point, though to our curious minds somewhat lacking in detail. He simply said, "You will surely die."

That should be enough to keep us a long ways away from trying to feast from this tree! If someone pointed to a delicious-smelling bottle of liquid and said, "If you drink this, you'll die," every one of us with healthy minds would promptly turn away. Or, if you were standing at the top of a cliff and someone pointed to the beautiful valley below and said, "Don't move toward it because the moment you do, you'll plummet to your death," would you promptly step off the cliff? Not if you're in your right mind. You'd back away, and the mere thought of stepping over that cliff would make your head spin.

That Adam and Eve were forbidden to eat from a source of knowledge does not suggest that there's something wrong with knowledge. All knowledge originates with God. The book of Proverbs highlights knowledge and implores us to get wisdom and get understanding. There's a proper place for knowledge. But only after we have feasted from the Tree of Life and ingested God's goodness into our beings are we able to handle knowledge. Jesus said, "They that worship me must worship me in spirit and in truth" (John 4:23). Notice the sequence? Spirit first, then truth. The Apostle Paul, in clarifying priorities, wrote, "Christ the power of God, and the wisdom of God" (1 Cor. 1:24). Again, there's an order listed, a proper sequence: power first, then wisdom.

Any church that is birthed from a lust for knowledge of good and evil will surely die. God has promised it so! But one that is born from a hunger for the very life of God will thrive. It cannot do otherwise, for it's His life at work. And it's a reproducing life. It's life that propagates itself in others. It multiplies like the living organism it is. It is born again and again and again in the lives of everyone around it.

The Tree of Life is where we feast. It is a place of worship. In fact, that's why Adam and Eve were cast out of that beautiful Garden of Eden—they got their worship wrong. They thought Satan was the one worth listening to (worthship = worship) when he slithered up to them and suggested God didn't really know what He was talking about. In his subtle way, he convinced them that such knowledge would be exactly what they'd need in order to survive in this world God gave them. He stoked their lust for knowledge—the knowledge of good and evil: "In the day you eat thereof you will be as gods, knowing good and evil" (Gen. 3:5).

While the Tree of Life is the place for feasting, the Tree of the Knowledge of Good and Evil is the place for following. It is the place of obedience. By not eating from it, we obey God. If we eat from it, we disobey. But disobedience was not the first issue; wrong worship was. Disobedience followed wrong worship. By worshiping Satan and thinking his word was worth listening to (worthship) instead of what God had said, Adam and Eve disobeyed. And they died.

The First Critical Concept for the Church

<u>Sequence</u>: What is causing your effect?

Two Trees
(Genesis 2 & 3)

. . . .

"Oh, that you would choose life, that you and your families might live! Choose to love the LORD your God and to obey him and commit yourself to him, for he is your life."
(Deut. 30:19-20, NLT).

Life
(Feasting)

Knowledge
(Following)

Worship ============> Obedience

●

●

| We are beings | ***Worship* is the path** | We are disciples |
| of <u>longing</u>. | ***to obedience!*** | in <u>learning</u>. |

<u>Power</u> ➡➡➡ 1 Cor. 1:24 ➡➡➡ <u>Wisdom</u>

"We have renounced secret and shameful ways; we do not use deception, nor do we distort the word of God. Instead, by stating the truth plainly we appeal directly to everyone's conscience in ways that are open and honest to God."
(2 Corinthians 4:2).

CONSCIENCE	INTELLECT
Adoration	Acknowledgment
Faith	Questions
Commitment	Dialogue
Spirit	Truth
Focus	Peripheral

And "as in Adam all died ..." so have we died too (1 Cor. 15:22). In fact, unless we are made alive again in Christ, we will never understand this simple principle of sequence, of putting first things first, just like Adam and Eve could not grasp it. Worship is the path to obedience! If we get our worship right, obedience will follow. But if our worship is wrong, it produces nothing but disobedience and doing things our own way. For a real church to be birthed, it has to be born from the Tree of Life.

Most churches struggle and die today because they are born from the Tree of the Knowledge of Good and Evil. They exist because someone got all hung up over a piece of knowledge somewhere, over some evil they were convinced should be avoided or some good they thought they could not live without. And so a church is born. But since they are feasting at the Tree of the Knowledge of Good and Evil, they are set up to die because God has said they would. Before long, and it's amazing how sure this is (then again, why are we surprised that God knows what He's talking about?), they are squabbling and scrambling around in the branches of the Tree of Knowledge because none of us have perfect knowledge or understanding of exactly what is good or of what truly represents evil. Before long, everyone is dead. They may still prop themselves up and mechanically go through some prescribed motions, but in reality they are dead, just like Adam and Eve died though they kept right on going through the motions of living.

Reflections in Marriage

6. The Propagation Pattern (Bride)

THE REAL THING:

One of the primary purposes of the church is to be reproductive/ evangelistic. The command Christ left ringing in the ears of His church was: "Go ye therefore and teach all nations" (Matt. 28:19a). This was the most important commandment, according to its timing.

I remember one time my parents getting into the station wagon and driving out the lane to be gone for several days on a road trip. They were all the way out to the road when I saw the backup lights come on, and my dad backed all the way up to the house where my twin brother and I were still standing, waving goodbye. My dad rolled down the window and said, "Oh, by the way ... don't forget to check the electric fences so the cattle don't get into the neighbors' corn." Then he rolled up his window and drove off again.

What do you think we remembered the most? Indeed! It was those final words left ringing in our ears. In the same way, the mere timing of the Great Commission highlights its importance!

In addition to The Great Commission, Paul's charge to Timothy was: "And the things that thou hast heard of me among many witnesses, the same commit thou to faithful men, who shall be able to teach others also" (2 Tim. 2:2).

<u>THE REFLECTION:</u>

God's primary purpose for the act of marriage was to reproduce children: "Be fruitful and multiply, and replenish the earth and subdue it" (Gen. 2:28). This command is given no less than four times in the first nine chapters of the Bible, once to Adam and Eve and three times to Noah after the flood (Genesis 8:17 and 9:1,7). It is also given later in the Bible. And never once did God even hint at altering this command.

Marriage is not an end in itself. It is a reflection of something much greater ... something eternal! The procreation of man is a reflection of Christ's final command to the church—to reproduce souls for His kingdom.

"How-Tos" For Couples

Loyalty: The Full End of Honor

Nothing grabs my heart more upon reflection than Rachel's loyalty. I still remember sitting in Eli Yutzy's living room in northern Minnesota back in 1984, on a date with the most stunning young lady I'd ever met; we were not even engaged to be married yet, but I asked Rachel, "How would you feel about someday being a pastor's wife?" I had sensed a call from the time I was young and felt she needed to know about that possibility. But I was apprehensive, because I didn't want to lose this lady! I can't recall her exact words, but I'll never forget the relief I felt when she assured me that if God ever called her to such a role, she was sure God's grace would be sufficient.

R = ___Relationships___ : Face to face in marriage; shoulder to shoulder with my friends.

A = ___Authority___ : The desire to serve and to lead is the essence of authority and manhood.

C = ___Conquest___ : God has put within every male image-bearer of Himself this chromosome.

H = ___Hierarchy___ : Something within the genes of a man longs to provide for and protect those under his care.

E = ___Esteem___ : Many women are shame-based in their approach to men. But this is the opposite of shame.

L = ___Loyalty___ : This is powerful to a man. An honoring woman believes in her man more than he believes in himself.

Not until after her death would I find out that way back when the children were young, Rachel had started a list of "Ten Reasons I Hate Being a Pastor's Wife." They were very good reasons … reasons every pastor's wife could list. Our teammates, Jared and Carmen, found that list when searching through her files in our home just days after her death while our family was in Colorado for Asher and Teresa's wedding. I knew Rachel had some notes on file for her own funeral should we ever need them. They eventually found the notes, and along with the notes, they also found this list of reasons Rachel hated being a pastor's wife.

At the top of the list was the consternation she felt from the tension of loyalties between wanting to be next to me in ministry yet also wanting to be at home with her children. Also near the top of the list was the fierce grief she felt whenever her husband came under attack for positions he needed to take in the work of the ministry. Her loyalty was overwhelming to me! She often believed in me even more than I believed in myself.

As a leader in our church and community, I sometimes experienced direct challenge and even opposition at times. It hurt her tremendously when I would come under fire, and she would grieve over my pain more than I did myself. But she was unflinching during those times and her faith in me never changed. We often marveled together at how some pastors were so self-conscious of what others think, and their wives sometimes even more so. They'd carefully nuance themselves so as not to lose any of their perceived following or invitations to speak at churches, or in protecting some semblance of their perceived reputations. It's really ironic because time has long since proven the truth without us even needing to worry about it—all because we were willing to let the political chips fall where they will. But Rachel was ALWAYS right there with me even though the risk to her was huge as well.

But for as significant as this loyalty was, and still is, to me, it was because of her loyalty to JESUS that Rachel is regaled in His royal presence today. I wish I could have been there to see her fall into His arms as she slipped away from mine. Simple acceptance is all she ever needed! She never tried to make an impression, but always left one. Bashful beauty, quiet grace, and gentle strength are expressions I hear repeatedly from those who try to describe her. And in my mind I always add: self-abandoning loyalty.

Because of such faithfulness to Jesus, Rachel is where she is today … high above us all in heaven with Jesus. But she is also famous here on earth within the hearts and memories of everyone who knew her. If you want to go where she went, follow her as she followed Christ and you'll end up where she is.

R.A.C.H.E.L. Not only did she put the R in relationships by her regard for mine, the A in authority by her attitude toward me and others, the C in her support for my conquests, the H in respect to hierarchy, the E in her esteem for who God made me to be, but even as Sarah of old who honored Abraham by calling him lord, she honored me in the same way and ended her life well by putting the L in loyalty—loyalty not only to her Lord, but also to me as her husband.

CHAPTER 16

The Beautiful Bride and Her Wedding Day

Rachel's Story

Brides are so beautiful! I always thought my wife Rachel was the most beautiful bride I'd ever seen! On October 20, 1984, we got married and traveled a most amazing journey for the next twenty-eight years and seventeen days. But those days were only a rehearsal. As you know, on November 6, 2012, Rachel went home to be with the Lord—her eternal Bridegroom, her forever Husband—JESUS. I wish I could have been there in heaven to see her fall into His arms that day as she slipped away from mine!

Rachel was a beautiful picture of how the Bride of Christ—the church—should honor her Bridegroom. Now I was not a perfect groom and didn't love her perfectly when she was here. Yet she still honored me and gave me leadership to her life as my wife. So much more should we as Christians, who are the Bride of Christ, honor HIM because He is a perfect Bridegroom and loves us unconditionally with a sacrificial love—He died on the cross for OUR sins. Imagine that! Now don't you think He deserves some honor from us in return?

Rachel left a legacy of honoring not only me as her leader and lover in the flesh, but also JESUS the eternal Lover of her soul. Rachel's story shows us how to fall in love with the Bride of Christ again. Wouldn't you be delighted to actually love the church again—the church that honors Christ? This is why she is regaled in His royal presence today. And this is why I tell her story. All she ever wanted to be on this earth was mine. And all she ever wanted US to be was HIS! Because of such faithfulness, she is where she is today … high above us all in heaven with Jesus. But she is also famous here on earth within the hearts and memories of everyone who knew her. If you want to go where she went, follow her as she followed Christ, and you'll end up where she is.

A rainbow arching over the intersection of
where the "accident" occurred.

Jewish tradition illustrates home-taking for brides so much better than our western weddings. There was roughly a twelve-month period of betrothal during which the fiancé was to prepare himself for marriage and to prepare a home for his fiancée. It was agreed upon and understood that the marriage would indeed occur, just not precisely when. This betrothal period had to pass before the marriage and the formal home-taking could be completed. At an expected, though inexact time, the bridegroom would suddenly appear at his bride's doorstep to take her home.[5]

When Rachel first accepted Christ, she became betrothed to Him until the preparation time was complete. At an expected, though inexact time, her Bridegroom came for her. She knew it could be at any moment. That's the way she lived … in ready expectation. No doubt, if given her earthly druthers, she'd have waited yet awhile, at least until after her son's wedding and maybe until all of her children were married, perhaps even longer. Yet though she knew for sure He'd come for her, she didn't know exactly when. It came as a surprise, both for her and for us!

I still stand stunned sometimes—the surreal significance of such a sudden change in circumstances—the betrothal behind, the wedding at hand. Yet that's really how we all must live, those of us who anticipate the imminent return of Christ our Bridegroom. Why are we so shocked? Is this not what we believe? And why linger in grief? Could there be a

---

[5]   JewishEncyclopedia.com

more marvelous move than that from earth to glory? Our long-expected marriage to Christ, the consummation of everything we believe. While it's staggering to us in our humanity, it's so clearly forthcoming to our faith!

And her happiness, oh her happiness! Is this not what weddings are about? While we may be jealous of what Rachel's enjoying, we can hardly begrudge her for her pleasure. Surpassing any wedding joy she'd anticipated for that Saturday was the overwhelming transcendence she'd gained on Tuesday. From worshipping Jesus at His footstool to casting her crown at His very feet! Exchanging wedding guest garments for bridal garments themselves. From merely the mother of a mortal groom to the royal bride of the King of Kings.

What a day it was! Friends and family who flew in for one wedding simultaneously took part in another. They called it a funeral, and it was. It was a farewell, it was sad, and it was final ... for now. But God always gets the last hurrah. What Satan meant for evil, God used for good and for His glory! Satan hates marriages and weddings, but God multiplied their

The "accident" site.

impact. Satan wanted to demoralize our family with the chaos, but God deepened our worship with new dimensions of His grace. What would have been one day of earthy wedding worship celebrating His goodness in this world became two days of heavenly wedding worship celebrating both His goodness in this life and His glory in the world to come.

Forever fixed in my memory will be the image of the little orange helicopter lifting up into the sky, carrying my dear Rachel away to the hospital in Colorado Springs. I had just kissed her on the cheek and said, "I'll see you soon." But no sooner had they lifted off when, according to the head medic of the transport crew, her eyes opened one last time, looked briefly around the Life Flight helicopter cabin, and closed again. And then her heart stopped ... but her spirit just kept right on winging its way upward into the very presence of Jesus, leaving her body behind to be carried on to the St. Francis Medical Center in Colorado Springs.

I would find her body there in the emergency room, still lying on the same stretcher where I had kissed her before they closed the door of the Life Flight helicopter. But it was not the same. Not only were there all kinds of tubes and paraphernalia attached to her body now, but her spirit was gone! I could feel the absence. The beauty of her spirit had fled the brokenness of her body. What appeared grotesque to me here in my earthly confines—her body without her spirit—was at that very moment in heaven a very beautiful thing ... her spirit set free. The real Rachel was not here anymore. Instead she was now free to be who she really was! As King Solomon had written, her "spirit return[ed] unto God who gave it."

Her Inspiration

The date was April 6, 2006.

It was the most thrilling dream I'd ever had. Rachel and I were young again—honeymoon-style young. I was at a place out in the country that was something between a wooded resort area and a farm setting. I was standing outside a big, widespread cabin.

All of a sudden, here comes a young, floating, swinging, bouncing, dancing lady towards me from out of the midnight sky. It seemed like Rachel, but it was more like her naked spirit. Not a sensual thing, but simply a wide open, free, nothing-hidden-sort-of-innocent-sense of naked transparency. She was running, swinging, dancing toward me in a way that said she wanted me to come. Like she was drawn and attracted toward me, yet at the same time she was teasing me along, flitting about, just out of reach in a flirting, enticing way, letting me know she was totally obsessed with me and wanted me to be totally obsessed with her. Then, as elegantly as she'd floated in from the sky, she floated away.

Then I awoke.

Could this have been some kind of premonition to me about her death ... the dance of her spirit between me and God, finally succumbing completely to Him?

The Bride of Christ

Second Critical Concern for the Church: <u>FOCUS</u>

In the previous chapter, we considered Sequence as the first critical concern for the church. The second critical concern for the church is the matter of <u>Focus</u>. Hebrews 12:2 says we should "look unto Jesus, the author and finisher of our faith." That means we need to keep our eyes fixed on Jesus. He needs to always remain the focus of our vision. There will be many other things that make up the peripheral part of our vision, too, but Jesus needs to always be the center of it all.

Paul the Apostle says he refuses "to know anything among [the Corinthian believers] except Jesus Christ and Him crucified." Now, as you may know, this same apostle went on to write nearly half of the New Testament. Obviously, he wrote about many other things than just Jesus. He wrote about marriage and families, he wrote about finances and how to manage them, he wrote about government, and he even wrote about how businessmen should conduct themselves. So it wasn't that he didn't think anything else mattered. It did. But he still said that when it came right down to it, he really didn't care about anything else except "Jesus Christ and Him crucified."

The early Anabaptist believers felt the same way. They were a people who experienced about as much persecution for their faith as did the first century believers in the Bible. The Anabaptists referred to the Outer Word and the Inner Word. The Outer Word made reference to the black and white pages of Scripture—the Bible. The Inner Word was a reference to Jesus Christ whom the Bible says is the Word of God. John 1:1 says, "In the beginning was the Word, and the Word was with God, and the Word was God." It goes on to say in verse 14, "the Word was made flesh and dwelt among us, and we beheld his glory, the glory as of the only begotten of the Father, full of grace and truth." This is an obvious reference to Jesus Christ. The Anabaptist believers felt that the ONLY value of the Outer Word (the Bible) was in its ability to lead them to the Inner Word (Jesus).

The first time I read that in Peter Hoover's book, *The Secret of the Strength,* I thought, "Wait a minute. I think the Bible has more value than just that." But the more I thought and prayed about it, the more I was persuaded that those early Anabaptists were right. What if I learned all about how to manage my finances, properly discipline my children, or love my wife but never learned to know Jesus Christ and Him crucified?

I'd go straight to hell when I die. So what good is all the rest? In fact, if I'm trusting in my knowledge of and obedience to all the rest, but never come to truly know Jesus, all those other great truths of Scripture only confound my heart and mind and keep me from really experiencing salvation through Jesus Christ.

If we could draw a series of concentric circles starting in the very center with a bull's eye titled "Jesus Christ and Him crucified" and then draw a cross right over that bull's eye and going out from there make this series of circles farther and farther out from the middle, it would give us something that looks like a target. The first circle out from the cross over the bull's eye we'd call "Central Truths." This would include such truths as the divinity of Christ, the virgin birth, the Trinity, the inspiration of Scripture, etc. The next circle out, we would call "Interpretations." This involves understanding what Scripture means. It's one thing to read what the Bible says, but it's another to really understand what it means. Certainly, good interpretation of various Scripture passages is critically important, but it's not as important as the simple truth of truly knowing "Jesus Christ and Him crucified." Out from there then, we could draw still another circle and entitle it, "Deductions." This would have to do with how we apply the Scriptures to everyday living. Based upon our interpretation of Scripture, we then draw some conclusions or deductions as to how we should live our lives. Again, it's important to make practical application of the Scriptures, but it's getting quite a ways out from the bull's-eye-importance of knowing "Jesus Christ and Him crucified."

The Second Critical Concept for the Church

Focus: Where are you centered?

Hebrews _12_:_2_   1 Corinthians _2_:_2_   1 Corinthians _3_:_11_   2 Corinthians _11_:_3_

"... the truth is in Jesus" (Eph. 4:21b). *Pilate asked "what is truth?" instead of "who" is truth!* (Jn. 18:38)

Conservative: Sticking close to the Scriptures.   Right-wing liberals.   Left-wing liberals.

Inner Word + Outer Word = Anabaptist view of the Scriptures.

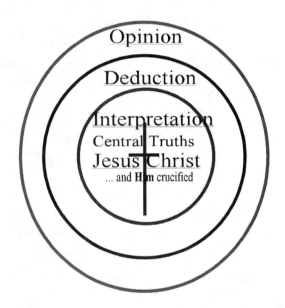

A wrong focus puts Christ in the peripheral! You cannot major on minors without minoring on majors!

"Problems in the Christian church experience are always corrected by a fresh revelation of Jesus Christ."
- T. Austin Sparks, The School of Christ

Still out beyond that circle yet we could make another one called, "Opinions." By now it's pretty obvious where we're going with this illustration. Of course, if you're going to have an opinion about something, have a good one. But honestly, I don't believe God really cares what my opinions are. What really matters are His opinions! We really need to be on guard about caring too much about other people's opinions. Yet many church systems get all caught up in highlighting all of their particular opinions about this or that or the other thing, and completely lost in the shuffle of it all is, again, the absolute imperative of knowing "Jesus Christ and Him crucified."

So the question the Bride of Christ needs to keep asking herself is this: Where am I focused? Am I truly focused upon Jesus, or am I focused on some lesser issue, something removed from the bull's eye? You see, the moment I focus somewhere out from "Jesus Christ and Him crucified," I have relegated Jesus to a mere peripheral part of my vision and made something else my focus. You can never major on minors without minoring on majors. You can't major on something other than Jesus without making Him a more minor part of your vision. Certainly the peripheral aspect of eyesight is necessary for healthy vision. Without it, we'd have tunnel vision and be constantly bumping into things because we failed to have a broad enough perspective. But without a proper focus, everything becomes blurred, confusing, and distracting. The peripheral always leads out from the focus, and, in turn, the peripheral always contributes back to the focus.

When Jesus stood before Pilate, Pilate asked him, "What is truth?" This probably seemed to Pilate like a pretty big question—that's why he asked it. But it really was missing the point. He asked the wrong question. We will never get the answers right, if the questions are wrong. If Pilate would have asked, "*Who* is truth?" he'd have discovered the answer standing right in front of Him—Jesus, the sum total of all truth. Ephesians 4:21 says, " ...the truth is in Jesus." Also, 1 Corinthians 3:11 says, "Other foundation can no man lay than what is already laid, which is Jesus Christ." The inversion of this Scripture reference is 2 Corinthians 11:3, where Paul says he's worried that, just like Eve was deceived by Satan, so the Corinthian believers' minds would be "corrupted from the simplicity that is in Christ Jesus."

Most Christians would like to believe they are careful keepers of the Word. But if we really want to be conservative in how well we honor and keep the Word of God, we have to do just that. We have to stick close to the Scriptures and not be compromised away from it either to the right or to the left. The terms "liberal" and "conservative" are rather nebulous, because they're subject to everyone's individual experiences. Perhaps a better definition for "conservative" might be: sticking close to the Scriptures. In light of this, I believe there are actually two kinds of liberals.

On the one hand there are right-wing liberals and on the other are left-wing liberals. A left-wing liberal is someone who takes a rather careless view of Scripture and relegates it off to some ancient time totally irrelevant from today. On the other hand, a right-wing liberal is someone who is so far into the other ditch, where they are busy trying to tighten up their applications to Scripture, that one can hardly recognize just what the real Scripture is and what they are trying to keep. Instead, let's be true conservatives and simply stick close to what the Scriptures really say, veering neither to the right nor off to the left.

T. Austin Sparks in his booklet, *The School of Christ,* says this: "Problems in the Christian experience are always corrected by a fresh revelation of Jesus Christ." My attitude should be that everything I think I know about God and His Word is "up for grabs" with Him. Not just with anybody, but certainly with Him! He can change my mind whenever He wants to! Not that I shouldn't be strong and stable in what I believe, but I must carry a humble, flexible attitude about my limited capacity to fully understand God, His Word, and His ways. My understanding is not "up for grabs" with men, although I should allow the insights of other dedicated men to influence me, but it must be God who changes my mind and my life. Personally, we should have nothing to hide, nothing to prove, and nothing to lose. It's all about God, not me.

Reflections in Marriage

7. The Reward of Faithfulness (Bridegroom)

THE REAL THING:

Christ is coming for His Bride, the church. Do you believe it?! Not maybe. He IS coming!

"And I John saw the holy city, new Jerusalem, coming down from God out of heaven, prepared as a <u>bride</u> adorned for her <u>husband</u>. And I heard a great voice out of heaven saying, Behold, the tabernacle of God is with men, and he will dwell with them, and they shall be his people, and God Himself shall be with them, and be their God" (Rev. 21:2,3).

THE REFLECTION:

The surety of Christ's coming is typified by the absolute faithfulness of the husband. Why does our culture live in such determined ignorance of the imminent return of Christ? Because the husbands of our culture have not been faithful!

"…these words are true and faithful. He that overcometh shall inherit all things; and I will be his God, and he shall be my son" (Rev. 21:5b,7).

"How-tos" For Couples

Seven Things HUSBANDS Should Stop Doing [6]

1. **Stop dishonoring your wife by criticizing her in front of your children or in public**. Marriages that knock each other all the time, even in good humor, are less than honorable marriages. Your kids need to see you modeling how to be supportive and complimentary, not critical, of your wife. And if you're serious about being a believer in Jesus Christ, you certainly know this isn't how Christ cherishes His Bride, the church. Nor will unbelievers be at all impressed with the One you claim to be worshiping. Please stop it!

2. **Stop comparing your wife to other women**. It's demeaning and devaluing to her. Your wife is created with immeasurable value and worth. Cherish her for exactly who she is, not for what she does or doesn't do. Remember, if you weren't married to her, you'd be married to someone like her because just as water finds its own level, so people of the same level of emotional health are attracted to each other. Besides, God's golden rule applies to marriage; do to your wife what you'd like her to do to you. You better stop giving her permission to compare you to other men.

3. **Stop trying to fix your wife's problems.** There, I just saved you a bunch of work. She needs you to listen to her … to let her go on and on for a while, describing exactly how she feels. If she needed the problem fixed, she'd have married either a plumber or a pathologist. I know, it's in our nature as men to want to fix things. So when Rachel used to tell me about some problem, instead of immediately sitting her down in my counselor's couch, I learned to lean toward her, look straight into her eyes, and listen. Try it. It'll stop most of your headaches too.

4. **Stop trying to control your wife**. In case your pastor forgot to tell you this before the wedding, wives aren't controllable. They want to be led instead. But following a good leader is an inside-out thing. If who you are doesn't inspire her toward you, then

---

[6] Inspired by and enlarged upon from Mark Merrill's blog: www. markmerrill.com

trying to get her to be just like you is going to guarantee years of unhappiness for both of you. As husbands, we need to let go of the reigns and allow our wives to be the lovers, mothers, and wonderful women God created them to be. Stop trying to control them.

5. **Stop being passive when it comes to disciplining and training your kids.** Becoming parents was a team effort; your wife didn't get pregnant by herself. And parenting continues to be a team effort throughout the entire lives of our children. It's not just Mom's job, especially when it comes to disciplining children. The Bible says, "Train up a child in the way he should go: and when he is old, he will not depart from it" (Prov. 22:6). The Hebrew word for "train" is "chanokh," which is the same word that the name Enoch comes from. Enoch walked with God. Walk with your children in the way they should go, and when they are old they will not depart from it. Stop loafing around and get with it!

6. **Don't be alone with any woman who is not your wife or related to you.** When I was married, before Rachel was taken home to be with the Lord, I had a personal policy not to spend time alone with any other woman. But if cause necessitated it, I'd always tell Rachel who I needed to be with, what we were going to be doing, where it would be, and how long. To do otherwise could have only invited unnecessary temptation into my life. So if you're not honoring your wife in this way, then you're dishonoring her. Stop it!

7. **Stop feeding your sexual desires from any source other than your wife**. Whether it's flirting with other women—such a stupid thing to do, by the way—or dabbling in pornography, avoid anything that could take your mind, heart, or body away from your wife. Treat your sexual relationship as something to be protected, not just enjoyed. Remember, the endorphins of sexual release resemble opiates and are addicting, so make your wife, not some sick substitution to her, your "addiction."

CHAPTER 17
Her Life Extended

Rachel's Story

When a woman takes up the risk of marrying a man, she extends her life through him.

"A risk?" you might ask.

Yes. From a human perspective, it is a risk. Aside from a God-created dependence upon him, a woman might rather save her life than risk it for a man. He's a human being, subject to weakness and failure. In spite of his best preparation and intentions, he could still disappoint. None of us are impervious to our own humanity. In reality, it's a mutual risk for men and women that hinges upon a mutual dependence. Jesus said if we try to save our lives, we'll lose them, but if we're willing to lose our lives for His sake and the Gospel's, we'll save them. So anyone who takes Jesus seriously is going to be willing to risk it all for Him. And that includes the call to marriage.

12/25/2012 05:58

A heart in the sand in honor of Rachel and my promise
to her of a hike along the beach on our 28th wedding
anniversary. We would do it after Asher and Teresa's wedding,
but she was killed four days before their wedding.

If we're believers, it should be a given that we'll be marrying "in the Lord." If we don't, then all bets are off—God is under no obligation to save our life if we lose it for something other than for Him and the sake of the Gospel. But if we're following Christ and seeking first His Kingdom, then He has promised that we will save our life by losing it for Him. End of story.

This is where Rachel was in her relationship with Him. She had surrendered her life to Jesus as a young adolescent. Furthermore, she had surrendered her natural desire for marriage to Him as well. But then, in turn, she also eventually needed to surrender the joys and freedoms of singlehood to Him. And it was a risk! She had witnessed others close to her whose marriages were struggling. Three months into our courtship, she wrote to her parents, "Ernest says he thinks our relationship has a future. Can a relationship that moves so fast, last?" With the encouragement of her parents and her own choice to seek God with all her heart, she chose to take the risk. And because of choosing risk over refuge, her life was reproduced in others.

Because she extended her life to include me, our lives have subsequently been extended through the lives of our five children, two daughters-in-law, and now three little grand-buddies. Plus, the influence of her life has been extended to even include the friends and associates of our children. None of this could have happened by Rachel saving her life and trying to salvage it from exposure to risk.

Our family photo at Marcel and Krista's wedding.

Her Inspiration

I just returned from the 2015 Minister's Enrichment Weekend in Harrisonburg, Virginia. The conference is put on every year by the Biblical Mennonite Alliance and hosted by various congregations across the country. One of the events of the weekend was a Ladies Tea, which ran simultaneously with the regular business session.

"Aren't women welcome at the business meeting?" you ask.

Of course they are. But, for some reason, the women seem to prefer tea parties. I wish I could have been there myself this year to hear some of the testimonies that were shared at the open mic. The lead-off question to the women was: "What women in your life has God used to speak His Word into your life?"

Throughout the weekend, various women came to me and said, "I think you'd be happy to hear what Ana Sanchez had to say about Rachel." Ana is the wife of Jose Sanchez, and she and her husband host our house fellowship services here in northeast Los Angeles. My teammates and I all agree that God's hand is on this couple, preparing them for leadership in our fellowship.

Our vision here at The L.A. ROAD (Real-life Opportunities and Discipleship) is to plant a network of house fellowships across the entire greater Los Angeles region. A few months ago, God began to lay upon my heart a sense for the vacuum that has existed here since Rachel's death over two years ago. Over time, this has become more and more obvious, and it eventually occurred to me that perhaps we should identify one of the ladies of our fellowship and call them into position to officially fill that role. Otherwise things kind of bump along by default, and circumstances dictate a least-common-denominator effect. Such an inadvertent dynamic always results in the compounding of human effort rather than the miracle of genuinely Spirit-led ministry. As I prayed over this dilemma, it dawned upon me that Ana should be the one called into this position. Just as this conviction hit my heart, it was like God said to me, "Why would you call only Ana into position to fill Rachel's place? Why don't you also call Jose into position to fill your place?"

"Dah!" I thought. "Why didn't I think of that?" Especially since our entire team would envision this someday anyway. Hence, I asked Jose and Ana to accompany me to the Minister's Enrichment Weekend, and Ana ended up at the ladies tea event where the question was posed, "What other women has God used to speak His Word into your life." I am told that Ana jumped to her feet and hurried to the microphone.

"Rachel's life is what spoke to me from God's Word," Ana said with tears streaming down her face. "Rachel never really said much," she went on. "Instead, she just lived it. And from the time I first saw her I thought, 'I want to be like that lady!'"

From the vantage point of being Rachel's husband for over twenty-eight years, it is clear to me that Rachel's mantle for this fellowship has fallen upon Ana. Among the sentiments of the other ladies expressing themselves to me about her testimony after their tea-time were these:

"It was an honor to meet Ana! She is a beautiful person inside and out. May the Good Lord bless her and keep her and her beautiful family!"

"Observing Ana and hearing her, I thought someday someone could have that same testimony of her as she had of your Rachel ... Ana glowed Jesus and peace!"

"Her testimony was so beautiful and full of heart ... When she saw Rachel, she saw Christ ... that's so awesome and precious!!"

Reflections in Marriage

7. The Reward of Faithfulness (Bride)

THE REAL THING:

The church will be forever united with Christ. "And the spirit and the bride say, Come. And let him that heareth say, Come. And let him that is athirst come. Even so come, Lord Jesus" (Rev. 22:17a, 20b).

THE REFLECTION:

The absolute faithfulness of the bride. "Blessed are they that do his commandments, that they may have right to the tree of life, and may enter in through the gates into the city. And they shall see his face; and his name shall be in their foreheads. And there shall be no night there; and they need no candle, neither light of the sun; for the Lord God giveth them light; and they shall reign for ever and ever. And I John saw these things, and heard them. And when I had heard and seen, I fell down to worship before the feet of the angel which shewed me these things. Then saith he unto me, See thou do it not: for I am they fellow servant, of thy brethren the prophets, and of them which keep the sayings of this book: WORSHIP GOD" (Rev. 22:14, 4-5, 8-9).

Conclusion:

Rachel always loved when I'd preach this "Reflections in Marriage" sermon, in part because of the illustration I'd use in conclusion. One summer when our family lived in International Falls, the city officials brought in a skydiver as part of a special event celebrating the completion of the construction of the biggest paper machine in the world (at the time). Hundreds of locals gathered in Smokey Bear Park at the center of the city to watch the skydiver land in a ribboned-off circle about fifty feet in diameter. Everyone was looking up into the clouds to see who would be the first to spot the diver after he jumped. Suddenly someone spotted him and there he was, gradually descending out of the clouds, down, down, down right into our ribboned-off circle. He landed with hardly a stumble.

While everyone was looking up, watching, I took a moment to look around at the site, and it was beautiful! Everyone's heads were lifted in expectation, and it made me think of Jesus' words to His disciples when He said, "Lift up your heads for your redemption draweth nigh." I pondered to myself at the time, and I still wonder, "What would it take to get our whole city to do just that—to lift up their heads in anticipation of the return of Christ!

The Bride of Christ

Third Critical Concern for the Church: <u>BALANCE</u>

In chapters one and two, we discussed the first two critical concerns for the church: sequence and focus. The third critical concern for the Bride of Christ has to do with balance. Christian truth is dialectical in nature—in fact, it would at times appear almost paradoxical. Our Bible is basically a Hebrew book. Even though the New Testament was written in Greek (the Gospels were initially communicated orally in Aramaic), the writers were Hebrew men. The Hebrew mind always expressed truth in terms of opposites by saying at the same time two seemingly contrary things. The final truth was found in holding both of these opposite truths together in balance—not rejecting one in order to accept the other, but accepting them both together. By doing so, each truth did not subtract from the other truth, but rather each added weight and meaning to the other.

This is true in many instances: (These are NOT opposites, but many times they seem to be.)

The Third Critical Concept for the Church

Balance: Are you properly weighing it all?

Truth in Balance

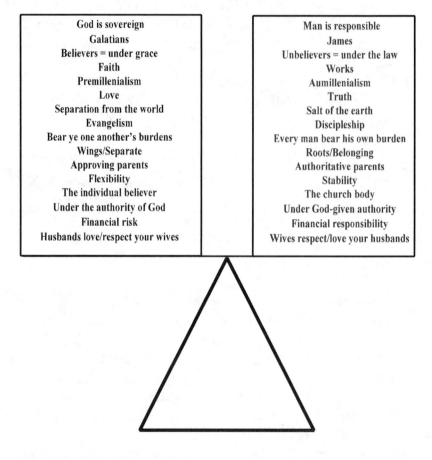

God is sovereign	Man is responsible
Galatians	James
Believers = under grace	Unbelievers = under the law
Faith	Works
Premillenialism	Aumillenialism
Love	Truth
Separation from the world	Salt of the earth
Evangelism	Discipleship
Bear ye one another's burdens	Every man bear his own burden
Wings/Separate	Roots/Belonging
Approving parents	Authoritative parents
Flexibility	Stability
The individual believer	The church body
Under the authority of God	Under God-given authority
Financial risk	Financial responsibility
Husbands love/respect your wives	Wives respect/love your husbands

Our problem as Bible students today is that we do not have Hebrew mindsets. We major in logic: if [(a = b) and (b = c) then (a = c)]. If this is true, and that is true, then this and that is true also. We emphasize one truth at a time. We try to make harmony out of *apparent* contradiction by either stressing one side or the other.

All too often we approach the Bible in the same way. We pick and choose whatever sounds the most *logical* and emphasize that. But we will never be able to understand real Bible truth until we are willing to adopt the Hebrew mindset and manner of thought—holding all truth together in balance. This is a fundamental concept! It is absolutely imperative that we understand it. Error has always crept into the church when we have refused to hold paradoxical truth together in balance. All of the earliest heresies of the church stemmed from the refusal of individuals to hold two seemingly opposing truths together in balance.

You see, the root meaning of our word "heresy" does not mean "untruth," but "half-truth." But it is "truth" taken in isolation–sundered from counter-truth—that produces error. Romans 1:18 and 25 talks about those who "hold the truth in <u>unrighteousness</u> (unequally)" and "change the truth of God into a lie." 2 Timothy 2:15 says " ...rightly dividing the word of truth," which means to make a straight cut, to dissect correctly.

"How-tos" For Couples

Seven Things WIVES Should Stop Doing [7]

1. **Stop putting others before your husband.** Successful living is a matter of sequence, of putting first things first. God needs to be number one of course, but since you've chosen to get married, your husband needs to be next. If you don't make your husband a top priority, your marriage will suffer. Do you really want to be part of a suffering marriage? How impressive is that?! Wives, give your husband the freshest and best of yourself, of your time, of your attention ... of everything. Stop giving him leftovers.

---

[7] Inspired by and enlarged upon from Mark Merrill's blog: www.markmerrill.com

2. **Stop expecting your husband to be your girlfriend.** If he was just another girlfriend, he'd be unnecessary and you probably shouldn't be married at all. He thinks differently than your girlfriends. He communicates differently. He processes things differently in almost every way. So don't treat him like a girlfriend or be exasperated if he doesn't respond to you as your girlfriends do. He's your complement, not your compliment. Not that he never compliments, but it won't sound like one of your girlfriends. That's simply not who he is. So stop treating him like one.

3. **Stop dishonoring your husband.** You won't readily recognize how you dishonor your husband, because you're not a man. But please allow me to awaken you to this natural blind spot that he may not know how to talk to you about. If you talk about him in a negative light to others, or if you talk to him as if he were a child or, worse yet, an idiot, he's not going to have warm feelings of affection for you. Be careful about questioning his judgment and abilities. And don't try to be his conscience. Men have an inborn tendency to resent their consciences. Stop giving him an excuse to resent you.

4. **Stop using sex to bargain with your husband.** Take your sexual relationship seriously. It's not a game. Nor is it an arm-twisting mechanism. It should not be used to get what you want. It's a very important part of your relationship. Jewish Dr. Laura used to pointedly ask her radio audience, "Why would you ever deny him something that takes so little time but makes him so happy?!" Sex is a given in marriage. Simply enjoy yourself and stop trying to make him earn it.

5. **Stop giving your husband your long term to-do list.** If he gets the impression that the list is endless, he may feel defeated and discouraged about helping you with the things that need to be done now. Keeping your "honey-do" list short-term means keeping it manageable and gives you frequent opportunities to celebrate together the projects you finish. If you don't, it may communicate that you're never content with anything he has done or will do. Good men truly like to make their women happy. Stop making it hard for him to do that.

6. **Stop requiring your husband to earn your respect.** Just as a husband should unconditionally love his wife, a wife should

unconditionally respect her husband. Of course that doesn't mean you need to like everything he does or agree with him on everything. And it obviously doesn't mean you should not address inappropriate behavior or actions with him. But it does mean that no matter what he does or says, you should treat him with dignity and honor simply because he is your husband.

7. **Stop expecting your husband to be prince charming.** If you keep expecting your husband to meet every dreamy expectation you ever had, you're bound to be disappointed and he's going to feel totally inadequate. As would you. Instead, focus on the things you do appreciate about him. Or if you insist on declaring him to be something he's not out of a desperate need for him to beat out the competition in your mind, your marriage will be very shallow. Newsflash—no husband is going to be the perfect prince charming of your dreams.

CONCLUSION

"Let us hear the conclusion of the whole matter: fear God and keep His commandments for this is the whole duty of man. For God shall bring every work into judgment with every secret thing whether it be good or evil" (Ecclesiastes 12:13).

There was a conclusion to Rachel's life here on earth. I still hurt because of it. She and I always recoiled when discussing the possibility of death for either one of us. But it's good we did; it was helpful in the end. She had a mere hour from the time of her accident until she was gone. I had a brief thirty minutes with her after I arrived on the scene. She spoke three words to me as I prayed for her: "Please help me." And so I did what I could, but her time had ended. Her life was in conclusion.

It was also the conclusion to our marriage. No more growing together. No more learning from each other or loving on each other. No more tender talks or conversations about our children and the journeys they were on. No more backrubs or tickling her ears or affectionately touching the tip of her nose. No more demonstrating by our life together at least a little bit of how much Jesus loves His Bride and how she gets along with Him. Such imagery had ended. The conclusion had been reached.

In like manner, the conclusion will someday arrive for that spiritual Bride, the church. Her time is limited. She does not have forever to fulfill her calling here on earth to live in demonstration of her Bridegroom's love for her. She has only this brief interval of time. Her conclusion is imminent as an earth-bound bride. In the meantime, she too moans out a desperate plea: "Please help me, Jesus!" And Jesus does, because He can! He has no limitation or conclusion, for He is the same "yesterday, today, and forever." He is everlasting! As our souls are linked to Him, they too will spring eternal, forever with the Lord, just as Rachel is today.

This gives us hope and purpose both in life and in death. Rachel's life was not in vain! It's laden rich with meaning and significance. She lives on in every one of us who knew her well, and even those who didn't, for she lived life not for herself but for her Lord and others. That's why I carry her story forward. Her life is worth repeating. And her children are living their own renditions of her life in their own versions.

That's also how the church's message will go forward. She does not gush in self-conscious obsession over her beautiful garments. Her Groom is all her glory! Nor does she waste His affection by a heart not linked to His, nor a life not lived for His purposes. Her radiant beauty is the reflection of her gaze into His face.

Rachel.

Our marriage.

The church of Jesus Christ.

All come to a conclusion here on earth.

But Jesus Christ lives on forever and supreme!

Our marriage to Him—Ah! This is our best conclusion!!

ABOUT THE AUTHOR

Ernest Witmer is an ordained minister in the Mennonite church. For over twenty-five years he has pastored churches in northern Minnesota and southern California where he now resides with his family in the Los Angeles community of Highland Park. He lost his wife Rachel—his bride of 28 years and 17 days—in a tragic car accident on the weekend of their second son's wedding in November 2012. Ernest and Rachel have five adult children: Carita, Marcel (wife Krista and son Judah), Asher (wife Teresa and sons Kenaz and Adrion), Kristi, and Christopher. His children and three grand-buddies are his constant delight.

Teaching from the Scriptures about marriage and family is a favorite for Ernest. He teaches in Bible schools, as well as church and youth camp settings, and does itinerant work in churches throughout the United States and in some foreign contexts. Ernest is an avid Facebook contributor and has written for Sunday school publications and Christian school curricula.

Ernest is currently the president of the L.A. ROAD (Los Angeles Real-Life Opportunities and Discipleship) ministry, a 501c3 non-profit in Los Angeles. The L.A. ROAD does house church development throughout Los Angeles and the Greater Los Angeles Surrounding Suburbs (GLASS). The L.A. ROAD also orchestrates an annual two-week Evening Bible Camp (EBC) in July and does systematic follow-up with a weekly Kids Club ministry year round.

Ernest does in-home marriage and family counseling, regularly meeting with couples and children from various church and non-church backgrounds and ethnicities. He is a certified administrator for the Taylor-Johnson Temperament Analysis profile and regularly facilitates seminars using the Caring for the Heart and Hope for the Family materials.

Not the least of all, Ernest loves to mentor men. He will give whatever time it takes to encourage fathers and sons, husbands, divorcees and their children to follow in the footsteps of Jesus to become sacrificial servant leaders in their homes, churches, and communities.

Ernest can be reached at **323-333-2279** or by writing to (or stopping by) **230 S. Avenue 55, Los Angeles, CA 90042**. His email address is: **ernestwitmer@juno.com**. He can also be contacted via: **https://www.facebook.com/ernest.witmer**.